Praise for Someone Has to Be the First

"Knowing Leslie as I do, and having worked alongside her for over two decades, I can tell you that this book truly reflects her spirit and journey.

Leslie's book is a powerful memoir that explores her experiences of often being the 'first' in various rooms and situations and the determination it took to navigate those paths. This early experience set a tone for her life, teaching her about resilience and speaking up when something isn't right. She's done it for herself, and she did it for me and my partners at FUBU.

For all of those who strive for greatness, you will often find yourself to be the 'first' in the room. Her insight and reflection will serve you well on this journey, as it has helped shape the man I am today. I know you will enjoy her authentic voice and unwavering belief that someone has to be the first, and that someone can be you."

– Daymond John, FUBU Founder, Shark Tank Investor

"Having known Leslie Short for more than twenty-five years, I've watched her transform every space she enters—with grace, conviction, and an unshakable sense of purpose. This memoir captures the power of a woman who went from trained ballet dancer to trusted advisor for organizations looking to expand their current culture. I learned so much about her and couldn't put this book down. From dance to fashion to corporate boardrooms, her life story is a masterclass in courage, reinvention, and leadership."

– Elena Romero, Assistant Chair and Assistant Professor, Marketing Communications, Fashion Institute of Technology

"Leslie Short is proof that courage and clarity can rewrite every rule. Her story isn't just inspiring—it's a roadmap for changing the world, one first at a time. For those of us who've had the great fortune to work with Leslie, she brings joy, compassion, and purpose to everything she does—and much like her life, this book uplifts and empowers."

– Jeffrey Sharp, Executive Director, The Gotham Film & Media Institute

"This memoir radiates resilience, courage, and hard-won wisdom. I was completely captivated, drawn in by every page, and reluctant to reach the end. It felt like a privilege to walk through the chapters of Leslie's life, witnessing the strength it took to go first, to forge ahead without waiting for permission or a path. Her honesty and heart are not only admirable, they're unforgettable."

– Kim Smith, Tech Executive

"There are so many lessons and bits of knowledge that would advance anyone if they could take that knowledge and process it the way Leslie has. I realized when reading the book that it doesn't matter what kind of opportunities are shown to you. Unless you can handle them, get it done, and keep it moving, it doesn't mean a thing."

– Mark Coughnenour, Former Dancer

"I am a firm believer in directed steps from God, and after reading *Someone Has To Be the First*, my belief is confirmed! From a young age, Leslie knew exactly what she wanted to do, and she put in the work to get there. From Chapter One to Chapter Thirteen, Leslie was not only first but also created an actionable plan to succeed!

I also believe that things happen in your life the way they are supposed to, meaning every path you take is your choice. *Someone Has To Be the First* is a smooth and easy read with clear points of direction that show how Leslie took advantage of every opportunity with a belief that she belonged in every room. Leslie is a pioneer of true success, and this book will also give the reader a blueprint to believe in yourself and never give up!"

– Joe E. Pryor Jr., Former Head of Security for Montel Williams and The Montel Williams Show

"*Someone Has to Be the First* is a beautifully written and heartfelt story about courage, discovery, and the power of embracing one's uniqueness. Leslie Short takes readers on an inspiring journey that begins with the innocence of a six-year-old second grader and follows her as she grows into a confident, expressive woman who learns to dance through life's joys and struggles and discovers her beautiful voice.

From the very first pages, you are drawn into her world of laughter, determination, and quiet reflection. You can almost see her dancing through the narrative, using movement as both a metaphor and a method for self-expression and resilience. Each chapter unfolds like a rhythm of life: sometimes fast-paced with excitement and triumph, other times slow and reflective, capturing the moments of challenge and transformation.

What makes this book truly special is its focus on finding your voice when you are different. Don't be afraid to step out. Leslie's journey celebrates individuality while honoring family values, relationships, and perseverance. One of the key messages that shines through is that every 'no' in life can be transformed into an opportunity to find another way. This message, both intimate and universal, will resonate with readers of all ages and backgrounds.

Whether you are a young reader just beginning to explore your identity or an adult reflecting on your path, *Someone Has to Be the First* offers encouragement to keep moving forward with faith, creativity, and confidence.

In the end, this is more than just a story—it's a celebration of courage, growth, and the power of being the first to step into the unknown. Thank you, Leslie Short, for stepping out first."

– Rev. DR. Joyce Brandon

"Through her work with our school, Leslie opened my eyes to topics I had not thought of before. She built relational trust and challenged existing mindsets. Her message shows how, if you are authentic and focused, you can succeed despite systemic barriers and roadblocks. I sincerely appreciate all she has done for our campus, helping our students access what they need and reshape our culture on campus."

– A. Michael Guyon, Educator

Someone Has to Be the First

INDIGORIVER
PUBLISHING

Someone Has to Be the First

LESLIE SHORT

Somebody Has to Be the First

Library of Congress Control Number: 2025926105

ISBN: 978-1-969935-22-0 (paperback) 978-1-969935-23-7 (ebook)

This book is based on true events reflecting the author's memory of them. Some names and characteristics may have been changed, some events compressed, and some dialogue recreated.

Editors: Sterling Hooker, Toby Israel, Abigail Dengler
Cover and Interior Design: Emma Elzinga

Printed in the United States of America
First Edition
3 West Garden Street, Ste. 718
Pensacola, FL 32502
www.indigoriverpublishing.com

Ordering Information:

Quantity sales: Special discounts are available on quantity purchases by corporations, associations, and others. For details, contact the publisher at the address above.

Orders by US trade bookstores and wholesalers: Please contact the publisher at the address above.

To my parents, who taught me that "no" is a complete sentence as well as an opportunity to do things differently.

To Henry, Dana, Francisco, Monique, and Michael—through your deaths, you gave me a different perspective on life and living.

Contents

Preface

I've often been the first—and sometimes the youngest—in rooms where no one expected me to be. Yes, history opened doors, but determination walked me through them. And still, I see people held back from their "firsts" because others don't want to make space.

Being the first isn't always glamorous. It can be lonely, exhausting, and full of silent battles no one sees. You're asked to prove your worth over and over again—not just for yourself, but for everyone who might come after you. You're told to be grateful for a seat at the table, even if the seat is folding and uncomfortable. And yet, you stay. You lead. You show up. Because you know that if you don't take that step, someone else may not get the chance.

Someone always has to be first. And sometimes, that someone is you.

I hope you find value in these pages. And I hope when you put this book down, you think to yourself, *There's more than one way to do whatever it is I want to do. And there's more than enough room for me to do it.*

I have drawn inspiration from countless people who have been the first and who have inspired me to do the work I do. Those firsts include people like Hattie McDaniel, Jackie Robinson, Shirley Chisholm, Colin Powell, Condoleezza Rice, Barack Obama, Sandra Day O'Connor, Rita Moreno, Misty Copeland, Ruby Bridges, Bethann Hardison, Ketanji Brown Jackson, and so many others. I hope my story pays forward the lesson their lives have taught me: First should never mean last.

Leslie

CHAPTER 1

New Jersey Is Not New York

I was about to go into second grade when we had the family meeting. We gathered at the dining room table as my father shared that he had been given two new job opportunities, one in California and one in New Jersey. He selected New Jersey because he would be able to help build a town.

Wait, what? I thought. *We're leaving New York? No, thank you. I'm good! I'm not moving . . . and did he say* town, *not city?* As a kid, I wouldn't have traded living in New York for the world. New York is culture, and I was lucky enough to be exposed to it through my family, friends, school, and even simply walking down the streets of NYC. It was common to hear different languages and see a variety of people everywhere. I was taught that no matter what someone has or doesn't have, no matter how they look, you treat them as you want to be treated. Respect is earned, not given, and if something is not right, you speak up. Those lessons have worked in my favor my entire life.

I was *not* feeling this move. *What about all the other things I do?* Back then, the education system had a variety of in-school programs for kids, from music and the arts to book clubs and sports, and I took advantage of them. And to make the idea of moving even worse, I had recently been selected to dance in a school assembly with an African dance company.

I knew it at age seven, and I know it now: I am a city girl. I can move anywhere, but deep down, I need to be able to move around, and not in a car. I need and want to have things happening around me—a diversity of activities and people—and something new to learn that brings me joy.

Let's be clear: growing up in the city had its pitfalls. One time, before my family's move, I had been out with my mom, sister, my mom's friend, and her daughters. I was carrying my purse with my Ring Dings (pastries) in it when a teenager ran past me and tried to steal my bag! He snatched it, but luckily, a man snatched it back and then yelled at him for trying to steal from a kid.

In New York City, just because culture and cultural outings are abundant, that doesn't mean people always blend across cultural lines. There are communities within communities, and some people don't cross those invisible cultural boundaries. They never see anything other than what they know. Still, there were countless opportunities to learn about other cultures for those with eyes open.

New Jersey was a different world from New York. The culture was different. Where we moved in New Jersey, people really didn't see beyond where they lived. The whole area was filled with trees and land, and we had to drive everywhere. Kids played with frogs and in the dirt; I wanted no part of it.

After we moved, I told my mom, "These kids aren't sophisticated. They don't know about pimps and prostitutes and the real world." I was only seven when I said that. If you were a kid growing up in New York in the '60s, '70s, or '80s, you knew about pimps and prostitutes. Times Square was not run by Disney.

The house in New Jersey was nice, and it wasn't an apartment building, but I still felt stuck inside it. My dad was busy building the town. He was one of the architects who moved to the area to help build housing developments. My sister and I needed a car to go anywhere, so there wasn't much we could do, as my mom didn't drive. She wasn't used to not being able to move around freely either. New Jersey is next door to New York, yet it felt so far away—the people, the town, all of it. We were in the country!

One day, once we had somewhat settled into living in New Jersey, I was playing outside as I often did. A woman who lived a few doors down came outside and said she had been watching me play the last few weeks. I explained to her my new skills: splits, flips, and turns. I said I invented them. She laughed (as she should have) as my mom came over. They began to speak, and I went along spinning and jumping. She told my mom that the Pennsylvania Ballet School was looking for little girls to train as classical ballet dancers, then asked if I would be interested in going. We yet didn't know that the woman used to be a modern dancer and still took classes.

"Of course," my mom responded, "Let me speak to my husband though because I don't drive."

My parents were not into the arts—my dad played softball, and I heard more about sports than ballet—but I was exposed to them. After talking with the neighbor, my parents agreed to let me audition on the condition that the woman ask me first if I wanted to go.

I was outside twirling and jumping when she came out to ask.

"Sure," I said, without missing a beat. I had no idea what I was saying "sure" to.

"I don't want you to get your hopes up," she said. "They don't normally train little Black girls as ballet dancers."

"OK," I said, and kept twirling.

Who knew that "yes" would change my life?

My mother couldn't drive, so our neighbor drove me from New Jersey to the audition in Pennsylvania. On the first day of the audition, there were hundreds of little girls dressed in pink with their hair in buns and their feet in pink ballet shoes. I did not have a leotard; I was wearing a purple bodysuit with snaps at the crotch! Now I wish I had held on to it. I think I was the only Black girl there.

There were mothers everywhere. When dance schools hold auditions for little girls wanting to start ballet, they want to see the mother too. That way, they can see what the little girls' bodies will look like as they mature. My mom hadn't come; it was just the neighbor and me. But if she had been there, I still would have been good, except for her breasts. My mom was billed as the Black Marilyn Monroe when she modeled because she had the same measurements.

I made it through the first body check and was put into a room to review my flexibility. The teacher lined us up against the ballet barre. One by one, they grabbed our feet, made us bend backward, stretched our legs, and pulled our arms, all while other teachers and directors looked on in the class and through the window. No parents, guardians, or other adults were allowed near the studio. I faintly remember little girls being escorted out. I was still in the room with my purple bodysuit.

Out of the hundreds of girls, they kept thirty for the second day of auditions. I was asked to come back.

∞

On day two, I arrived again with my neighbor and my purple bodysuit. We were broken up into small groups, since there were only thirty of us. Out of those thirty, the school was only going to pick three girls.

My name was called, and I went into the studio. Once again, the teachers stretched me and then asked me to follow their directions about what to do with my feet, legs, and arms. I followed without issue. Then they left the room, saying, "We will be back shortly." Some girls sat and talked, and others played on the barre.

Me? Well, I needed to show them what I invented.

I started jumping in the air, doing my splits and twirling as I told other girls to try it. I lined them up and had them follow me. I had no idea the teachers were watching us to see how we interacted with each other. They came back into the room and said, "Thank you. We will let you know in a few days."

I didn't think much about it. All I knew was that I had fun and got to show others my jumping splits. On the way home, my neighbor reminded me not to get my hopes up. She told me that I should be proud that I had done well, especially since I had never taken a dance lesson.

A few days later, I received the call. Out of the thirty girls, I was one of the three selected for training. I still didn't understand what it meant to be trained as a classical ballet dancer, other than that I would learn how to do bigger jumps in the air.

I did know it wouldn't be easy to get to class. *How will I get to Pennsylvania three times a week?* I wondered. My mom was still not driving, the neighbor couldn't possibly take me that often, my sister was in school running track and doing band, and my dad was building the town!

My parents promised we would make it happen, and we did. Or the universe did. One of the lead teachers from the Pennsylvania Ballet School, Ms. Haught, was retiring and opening a school in New Jersey, which would still be affiliated with PBS. She had a studio. It wasn't the PBS studio, but I was going to learn to dance there. My neighbor could commit to taking me to the studio in New Jersey three times a week.

Seems like New Jersey will have something to offer me after all, I thought. Time would tell.

By the time I started at the studio, I was ready. I was official this time, with a pink ballet leotard, tights, ballet shoes—and of course the ballet box to hold my shoes, towel, and everything else. I walked in and changed, and Ms. Haught lined us up at the barre. There was a piano and a piano player.

Ms. Haught looked at all the girls and started reciting the rules.

"You must not chew gum, your hair must always be tied back in a bun, and you must wear pink," she said. We learned that pink was the color for beginners, and we would change leotard colors depending on our level or scholarship. "You must be on time," Ms. Haught continued. "No playing around."

Great, I thought. *Let's go.*

She came to me and said, "You must take your bracelets off."

When we lived in New York City, our next-door neighbor from Jamaica had given me sterling silver bangles that were supposed to bring me good luck and told me not to take them off. (I do not remember taking them off for the audition, but I must have.) I didn't think twice about keeping my bangles on when I changed into my ballet clothes for class.

I can still remember standing near the piano. "No, thank you," I said.

"No jewelry is allowed in class unless they are stud earrings," she explained again. "No rings, bracelets, or necklaces. It can be dangerous."

I still said no, explaining that they were given to me as a blessing, and I had been told not to take them off.

The other girls stood there watching this exchange. I was taking up class time. Clearly, we were at an impasse. *Maybe dancing is not for me.* I thought about saying goodbye.

I don't know why Ms. Haught was patient with me, but she looked me in the eye and said, "If you take them off, I will put you near the piano, and the bracelets will stay on the piano where the piano player and I can see them. Would that work?"

I reluctantly took them off and placed them on the piano, their usual spot for years to come.

I learned many things from Ms. Haught. I grew up in her studio and moved through ballet levels. When I wasn't in class, I watched the older students dance and knew without a doubt that was what I wanted to do.

New Jersey had three places where I really felt at home. My home, the ballet school, and church.

I went to the Baptist Sunday School, and I loved it. I took the blue bus there since my family went to a different church. Sunday school meant learning and being peaceful.

One day, at the end of class, the teacher asked if there was anyone who would like to accept God into their lives, and then she explained what it meant. I was so excited. *Yes*, of course I would accept God into my life. In my seven-year-old mind, I thought, *If there is someone bigger than all of us who will watch over me as I go through life, then I'm in! I know I will need him; this dancing thing is going to be hard. Plus, they keep saying dancing can be very lonely. Well, not for me*, I assured myself. *I'll have God.*

I was dancing five or six days a week and loving it, but just in case it didn't work out, I would ask God each night in my prayers if I could come work for him. In my mind, I had to be a nun to work for God, so I wanted to become a nun. As part of my prayer, I'd ask, "Dear God, how can I come work for you? If I can come to work for you, do I have to wear the same outfit each day? Can I change it up with jewelry or shoulder pads? Thank you, God. Love, Leslie."

I still laugh because God laughed and said, "I gave you the talent to dance. Do that, and maybe I'll call you later."

CHAPTER 2

It's All About Dancing

When people ask what the most formative years were in my life, I say seven because of dancing and God, and twelve because that was when I became a professional ballet dancer.

At twelve, I was learning pointe (where you dance on your toes). My mom had learned how to drive and was now bringing me back and forth to class six days a week. It was my mom who would pick me up from school each day as I ate half of a sandwich on the ride from New Jersey to Pennsylvania. I would be in class until around 7 p.m., drive back to New Jersey to do homework, then start it all over the next day.

People began to tell my parents I would most likely quit between the ages of thirteen and fifteen. When girls discover boys, they want to hang out with friends and go to dances, those people said. Five or six days a week of ballet class and going to school was a lot. I did not hang out, and it was rare that I went out with school friends. I was already focused, and I was turning professional. (Yes, I was paid for some of my performances.) I was not dancing lead roles yet, but I was getting small solos and receiving invitations to dance in certain ballets. When I was older, I had two ballets created for me, and I began dancing lead roles.

Around this time, one day set the tone for the rest of my life. My parents had given me a strong foundation of self-worth, purpose, ethics, and love, but it was Ms. Haught who pulled me aside and taught me a different type of work ethic that I have never forgotten. I was playing around and laughing in class with two of the other girls. After class, Ms. Haught looked me in the eye and said, "Don't you ever play around in class again. You are very talented, more than the other girls, but their parents will pay their way into a company." She was referring to the way many girls' parents would make substantial donations to assure their daughter got a spot, regardless of the girl's ability or behavior. "Your parents will not do that," Ms. Haught warned. "Not because they can't, but because they won't. They'll expect you to *earn* your spot by working hard and staying focused."

After that day, I knew there was a time to work and a time to play. Dance was work.

Saying I was a ballet dancer as a little Black girl had some folks on their heads. Kids didn't understand it, and adults thought my parents were crazy to let me run back and forth to dance class each day. Weekends were for the next-level classes and rehearsals. That meant I needed to quit gymnastics and cheerleading at school, because there was no way I could do it all. I still went on a few class trips and somehow did a few activities with classmates, but if it wasn't about dancing, it was not important to me. That included school.

I was a good student and a bad test taker. I used to pray to be smart like many of my friends who were on the honor roll. I didn't want to be on the honor roll; I just wanted to be smart in a test-taking kind of way. I knew I was smart in different ways, but with that piece of paper in front of me (yes, paper), all I wanted was to be in the dance studio. I had my career.

I had many teachers who were supportive of my dancing and would make sure I had the assignments I needed when I went on tour or had to take a few days off to perform. In sixth grade, when I walked into the classroom on the first day, I saw that the teacher had a huge decorative sign that said "Dynamite" hanging across the front of the room. The entire room was decorated as well. I was excited, thinking I was going to like her.

That changed quickly, as it was easy to see she preferred the white students over the Black students. It was her tone when she responded to the white kids. They would get a laugh, while the Black kids would get a half-smile. So, she wasn't going to be my favorite. *Whatever*, I thought. *I have several performance dates coming up. I'm just in school because my parents say I have to go.* My parents wouldn't send me to a private boarding school for dance because they were told it was not as serious as the dance classes I was already receiving, nor would I have the same opportunities to dance and study with various teachers. *Looks like I'll be in a cool, decorated classroom with a not-so-cool teacher. Jesus, take the wheel!*

I remember going up to my teacher with a note from my parents about the days I would miss. Everyone knew I performed. The local papers had featured me, and the other teachers were supportive.

When I went to speak with my teacher, however, she said, "I don't care about the note."

"Excuse me?" I responded.

"You're being silly," she said.

"Silly or not, please take the note from my parents."

"Well, I'm not honoring it."

"Great," I said. "The principal will." And he did.

Another time, the same teacher made a comment asking why I didn't take gym class.

Here we go again, I thought.

"I have a note that states I meet the gym requirements because I train five to six days a week as a dance student and a professional dancer," I explained.

This time, she snapped. In front of the entire class, she roared, "Tell your mother to stop sending you to school like you're going to a fashion show. She should stop putting fantasies in your head because there is no such thing as a Black ballerina!"

I stayed in my seat, but I was fuming. I shot back, "Who do you think you're speaking to? And why do you think you can yell at me like that?"

Finally, I jumped out of my seat and headed for the door as she kept yelling about how there was "no such thing as a Black ballerina."

When I get mad, I cry. And if I cry, watch out. I looked at her from the doorway and said, "You will regret this."

I went to the pay phone in the hallway and called my dad in his office. He was not there, but his business partner, Jason, was. Jason was like a second dad to me, a Southern man who took no mess. He could hear that I was upset and said he was heading to the school.

I called my next-door neighbor, Jack, next because I couldn't get my mom on the phone (this was before cell phones and pagers). He was a college professor, and he lived with the woman who took me to the ballet audition. As a kid, I thought Jack was in his own world. He would always say, "I want to go sit on a mountain and just be." Lucky for me, he wasn't thinking about his mountain that day! Jack said he was on his way.

In the meantime, other teachers heard me crying and started coming out of their rooms. I told them what happened and said, "She will be sorry for the disrespect. I don't care if she is a teacher!"

They tried to calm me down as a male teacher went to my classroom to see what had happened. Jack and Jason arrived, one behind the other. Jack reached the teacher first after I walked him to the classroom. He opened the door and asked her to step out immediately.

Before I knew it, Jack and Jason had surrounded her with Jason stating, "If you ever speak to Leslie that way again, it will be the last time you teach a child."

"Don't hurt her," the male teacher said, trying to keep things calm.

"There's no need for that," Jack and Jason both said. "But clearly she was confused about who she was yelling at. If Leslie ever calls or comes home with another story like this, it will be our issue."

I should mention that both Jack and Jason are white. I think that, and the fact that the two of them showed up—and so quickly—threw my teacher more than anything. They told me to get my bag; the day was almost over, and my mom would be picking me up to go to ballet.

Keep in mind, this was a different time. I still have no real explanation for why she yelled at me so violently, other than that she said she was sick of me getting special privileges. That, and that she truly didn't believe a Black ballerina did (or should) exist. I bore the consequences of that disbelief. I was not the first, and I was not the last.

Most of my classmates treated me kindly. Still, in school, there are always going to be a few who just don't like you. I don't believe I thought I was better than anyone else; it's not how I was raised. I just knew that I was already focused on my career, and I was able to do things differently than my classmates. I worked hard to go to school and stay on top of classes, rehearsals, and performances.

The ones who did not like me came at me. I was called stuck up, BAP (Black American Princess), Rich Girl, and my favorite, Oreo. It means exactly what it sounds like: Black on the outside, white on the inside. I wasn't Black enough for some of the Black kids because, just like that sixth-grade teacher, they thought there was no such thing as a Black ballerina. They thought I was acting white, talking white, and dressing white. They believed I was stuck up because my family had money and that I was the teacher's pet—which I clearly was not. Well, at least not for my sixth-grade teacher. For some of the white kids, they never said anything to my face, but I could feel the judgment coming from their parents.

I had two close friends at school. One invited me over for Shabbat dinners and presented me with my first Star of David. That friendship was the start of my understanding and curiosity about Judaism. My other friend had nine brothers and sisters, so what was one more kid at the table? Except, I was the only Black kid. Her dad never said, "No, she can't come over," yet sometimes saw the look on his face seemed to say, "It's okay if she doesn't come over." I still went when I could. She was my friend, and that was that.

One day at school, a boy was picking on her. I took my pocketbook full of rocks and swung at him to make him leave her alone. I should mention I was not a big kid; dancing stunts your growth. Yet what I didn't have in height and weight, I made up for with my pocketbooks, which always matched my outfit, and where I also had my wallet, lip gloss—and rocks. I had no intention of fighting, but I was always prepared to give one good swing if needed.

I tried to be involved in school as much as I could, participating in student government or cheerleading. But I would always end up leaving because I was going on tour, or because the performance schedule was heavy. Some kids understood, while others felt I was treated differently. To a certain extent, I was. I knew I had privilege—and privileges that came along with the privilege. I like to think we all have a degree of privilege; it's the privileges that separate us. I knew if a kid came at me teasing, a teacher would shut it down. I knew I thought differently than the other kids did; most of the people I was around were older dancers and stagehands. I was usually the youngest dancer performing outside of Nutcracker season. On tour or at rehearsals during the rest of the season, I was the youngest and most likely the first and only Black person within that circle.

Beauty pageants were the other activity I would take part in between rehearsals, school, and performances. As if the kids didn't have enough to say, there I was, squeezing in a beauty pageant.

Dance was my talent. I remember that at one pageant, a judge asked me, "What did Mr. Balanchine say about dancers?" (Mr. Balanchine was a choreographer, regarded as the father of American ballet.)

I looked him in the eye. "He said a dancer should be the color of an apple core. But that's not the color I am, so what he says doesn't mean much to me."

The judge just sat there. As far as I was concerned, I was asked a question, and I answered. Next question.

Growing up around dancers and dance instructors coming at you from all different angles gives you two options: be strong or melt away. I never thought about melting away.

Most days, I would eat dinner in the car. Dinner consisted of a salami and cheese sandwich, which I would only eat half of on the way from New Jersey to Pennsylvania. I couldn't eat much before my first ballet class. I'd take a class or two at one dance studio; then, we would get in the car and drive to the next company, where I would take a class and rehearse for an upcoming performance. Rinse and repeat, except weekends. I didn't have school, but I would still dance. Around the age of thirteen or fourteen, I started staying at one of the older dancers' apartments (by older, I mean eighteen or nineteen) so I could be at an early morning class on Saturday, followed by a full-day rehearsal. It gave my mom a break from driving.

I was running around between three different dance companies at that time and never noticed the pain. There was always something hurting. My knees were always in pain, and I lived with ice packs on them most days. I was also in physical therapy at the University of Pennsylvania. In the clinic, I was the only ballet dancer getting worked on between two huge professional football players. The three of us would discuss the pain and rehab together. Pain was common, just part of the job.

One day, my mother came to pick me up from the Nutcracker rehearsal and asked me why I was limping across the stage. I had no idea I was limping because no one—and I say this with all my heart—*no one* in ballet cares if you are limping. "Get it together and do it again," was the only encouragement I received. I was lucky I picked up choreography fast; if I couldn't get it right during rehearsals, I would dream it that night and be able to dance it the next day.

My mom forced me to go to the doctor, and it turned out I had a hairline fracture. I began to explain to the doctor how he needed to wrap it, since I needed to get back to rehearsals. I did not leave the doctor's office with a wrapped foot, but in a cast and crutches. The three months that followed were the longest of my life.

Overall, I have good memories from school. But despite all the supportive teachers, the one I remember most was the sixth-grade teacher who told me I couldn't and wouldn't. I knew she was wrong, because I was already doing what she said I couldn't do.

Years later, I was featured in a three- or four-page magazine story. One of the African American teachers at my former school bought several copies of the magazine and displayed them all around the teacher's lounge to make sure my sixth-grade teacher saw it. To the new teachers, she was sure to state, "This is one of ours. She was here and already had a career, whether some wanted to acknowledge it or not." I had no idea, but that day in the hall left a wider impact than I thought. And I had no idea what adventures were still ahead of me.

CHAPTER 3

No Apologies for My Glow

Who knew a day trip back to New York to take one ballet class, eat lunch, and shop at Barney's would be a change-making day in my life? It was a day off from school, and my parents decided that we would drive up to NYC so I could take a class with the Joffrey Ballet School. We would then meet my dad's friend for lunch in Chinatown, and to close out the day as usual, we would shop at Barney's with my dad, where he would "suggest" we head to the women's floor on the penthouse level.

After the class at Joffrey, I was asked to stay and take the pointe class that was happening in an hour. I checked in with my parents, and they were fine with it. After the second class, the administrators asked my parents if I was there to audition for a scholarship, because technically, they were full. We said no; we knew nothing about a scholarship or the prior auditions.

There was a bit of discussion behind closed doors. Then the administrators returned, offered me a partial scholarship, and handed us a list of boarding houses for young ladies. I would need to be back in New York in two months.

My parents and I looked at each other, surprised. But I had learned from my parents to keep it moving, and that we did! We made arrangements to assure I could be back in two months. Instead of immediately going to lunch as planned, we visited the three closest boarding houses next to the school, which at that time was located on 10th and 6th Ave. We looked at Milbank House, Katharine House, and Markle Residence.

I wanted Milbank House, a beautiful brownstone with only thirty-two girls, but it was already full. Markle was also full, but I got into Katharine House on 13th Street. I was lucky to get a single room, since they had eighty-two girls, most in shared rooms. My room had a bed and a small sink; shared bathrooms and phones were down the hall. The boarding house residents were a mix of young women, some going to college or prep school, and others working in fashion or as models, dancers, or actresses. Ages ranged from thirteen to twenty-eight. Everyone was living in New York, chasing their dreams.

The day I moved into Katharine House, my parents drove me from New Jersey. The room was small and bare, but I had everything I would need, plus some, like my own TV. I had money in my pocket and all the tights, ballet shoes, and pointe shoes I thought I would need. I settled in, then we went to lunch and said our goodbyes. I was officially living back in New York at the age of fifteen. *I'm ready,* I thought. *A little scared, but ready!*

I moved in on a Sunday, so it was relatively quiet in the house. After my parents left, I went to the library/living room area (picture *Downtown Abbey* era), where a few girls were stretching on the floor—clearly dancers.

"Why are you here?" They asked me.

"I'm on a scholarship with Joffrey," I stated proudly.

In my head, I was laughing at how they scanned me from head to toe. They stared at me like crazy, clearly wondering how I got a scholarship.

"Well, stay away from those girls over there," they said, motioning to a handful of other dancers milling about the common area. "They aren't on scholarship *anywhere*."

Dancers from Joffrey, ABT (American Ballet Theater), and SAB (School of American Ballet) were rivals. Other girls were dancing in other places, but if you weren't at one of the "top three," you were a bit of an outcast.

I didn't take the girls' advice, and I spoke to anyone I wanted. There was only one other Black girl living in the house, and she was also a dancer at Joffrey. I don't remember her caring about who others thought she should speak to or not. She was very much like me in that sense. She'd moved into the boarding house the summer before, so maybe she never got the "don't speak to them" speech. She'd been there longer and moved how she wanted.

On my first day of classes at Joffrey, I selected a place at the barre, and that's where I stayed for the next four years. I remember being placed in the center of the second line behind a dancer whose leg was beyond her ear, which meant mine needed to do the same, if not more. Where you are placed on the barre and in line to dance across the floor is a big deal. Dancing is not a team sport, and dancers compete against each other every day. In fact, it's encouraged.

I remember how the girls from California with flowers in their hair were treated differently than the rest of us; the European dancers could do no wrong. I also remember the diet pills that most of the front row took to stay under 100 pounds, and most of all, I remember that there were three Black dancers:

two girls, including myself, and one guy. For the four years I was there, there would only be three Black dancers, regardless of how many students came on a full or partial scholarship.

Spending my summer in New York at age fifteen was amazing. The week was full of classes. My first ballet class started at 9:00 a.m. I would wake up before 7:00 a.m. to watch the Today Show, then go downstairs for breakfast, which meant maybe having an apple or muffin. Mondays were weigh-in days. You could not be heavier than the week before. Being called fat was common. Eating, not so much. Since there were other dancers in the boarding house, everyone was watching what the others ate. The competition was no joke; just because you got in didn't mean you would stay in. I saw girls pass out and get sent home because of weight, drugs, or alcohol.

I was focused on Monday-to-Friday classes, which were over around 5:00 p.m. On Saturday, classes ended by 2:00 p.m. After Saturday classes, I would run back to the boarding house, change, and go have my hair washed on Eighth Street. That was the one day I would wear it down and not in a bun.

Eighth Street in the '80s and '90s was everything—funky and fashionable, full of little restaurants and great shops. It was NYC, the Village, and I was in the heart of it. Besty Johnson's store, Patrica Fields, Capezio. Going to Eighth Street was an *event*. The Black hair salon I went to was full of celebrities, and I was the little ballerina who they made a fuss over whenever I came in. They appreciated the fact that I was in NYC to dance ballet. They had mainly only ever seen white girls going into the Capezio dance store across the street.

I saw some things at fifteen that a lot of people haven't seen in their lifetimes. I made great friends, one of whom, Susan, is a dear friend to this very day. Technically, we shouldn't have been friends. She was SAB, then she went over to ABT, so we were rivals in the attitude of being dancers. Dancers from different schools, companies, and genres can be snobby! Susan was from a small Virginia town and extremely Southern. New York was new for her, but not for long. Meanwhile, I was back where I belonged; in New York I was home. She was quieter than I was, and neither of us now can remember how we started talking. We spent two summers at Katharine House and hung out a lot the first year, going to the supermarket because the boarding house had no air conditioning. We'd sneak out to eat at Entenmann's cakes and Ray's pizza on Sundays.

My first summer flew by. I was invited to take classes during the winter, but my parents made me come back to New Jersey and finish out eleventh grade. Whenever I had a school break and I wasn't performing with the other companies, I would come back to New York for class. I was again invited back for a summer scholarship, and I was happy since I knew Susan would be back too.

Back in New Jersey, my routine of being driven from class to rehearsal to a different company only became more intense. I was performing a lot. At fifteen, I was already dancing with a different ballet company, and I had gotten into Philadanco, which was not ballet! Philadanco was a modern dance company with some of the best teachers from Alvin Ailey and the Dance Theater of Harlem, along with guest teachers. It was also a predominantly Black company. At that time, I was the youngest person to make the main company. Lord, that was the first time I saw or took a class full of Black dancers. Philadanco taught me a lot, and I am grateful to Aunt Joan—that's what we called the owner and creator of Philadanco. They teased me about ballet, but they took me into the company and embraced my presence there.

Philadanco may have been the first and only "Black" company I performed with. I still love to watch Alvin Ailey and the Dance Theater of Harlem (DTH) perform in NYC. I was accepted into DTH that same year, but my parents would not let me move to Harlem by myself and felt that the boarding house was too far for me to be on the trains at night. Plus, they wanted me to finish my last year of high school in school, not with a tutor. So back to New Jersey I went for the school year, and back to New York for the summer.

My second year in Katharine House was uneventful. I still didn't like the food; I was lucky that one of the women who worked in the kitchen was still there. She was an African American woman, and she noticed I barely touched my food (though anyone who was a dancer barely touched their food). We were given two meals a day and brunch on the weekend, and we could not have double servings of anything. The only thing that I really liked was their blueberry muffins, and bless her, she would sneak me an extra muffin so I could take it to my room. I always think about that kind gesture. Technically, she could have been fired, but she still made sure I could have at least one more.

Don't be too concerned, thinking I did not eat at all. I ate, I just never had full meals. I ate to pass the weigh-in each Monday. If you watch dancers eat, you may never want to eat again. There is always the one who takes every bite like it's her last. Another eats slowly, then pours salt or pepper all over the plate and covers it with a napkin. There is the one who eats everything, but you know she is going to go upstairs and vomit. You have the two-bite girl who then shoves her plate away, or my favorite, the girl who does not let food touch her lips. If I didn't like something, I didn't eat it. I was that way then, and I still am now. Food, to me, was not my friend—it simply served a purpose.

When I was growing up, my parents didn't say what other parents said all the time: "Be careful around boys. Don't drink or smoke." Instead, mine would ask, "Did you eat today?" They knew that the other stuff would not have a chance if it got in the way of dancing.

My senior year of high school, I was invited to stay for the winter again at Joffrey, but I went back to New Jersey, where I saw an announcement for an audition for the Nutcracker for a regional ballet company. I auditioned and received various parts. Snowflake, Flowers, and the Solo of Arabian. All good parts; of course, the solo is always what you want. There was a bit of an uproar with the parents. How dare the school give major parts to an outsider *and a Black girl* when they pay money for their little girls and boys to attend the school, they complained.

For some reason, the director, the same woman who accepted me into the season and awarded me the parts, had issues with me. I think it was the pressure of the paying parents and the fact that many people said I danced better than her daughters, even though I was younger. I don't know, but I do know that her issue with me reared its head during rehearsals for Snowflake.

During one rehearsal, she was yelling at all of us to smile and for our faces to be pleasant when she yelled, "Leslie, you stop smiling. Your teeth are messing up the lights."

I was the only Black dancer who had danced with them. Regardless, I kept going, and as I went around in the circle, I said, "You have never seen snow in New York. It turns black quickly."

Needless to say, she was not thrilled, and she went off on a rant. I walked off the stage, picked up my dance bag, went to get changed, and started walking down the dark wooded road. Her husband ran after me. "Sorry," he said. "Please don't go. She was wrong for saying that to you."

At the same time, my mom was driving up and saw me. "Why the heck are you on the road?" she shouted from the window.

I started to tell her as the husband ran up to the car, apologizing to my mom. "Please, Leslie, wait a minute," he said.

My mom was confused. "Should I come in?" she asked after she parked the car.

"No need," I said. "I don't know what they can say to me."

What they did say was sorry. I went back, even though I didn't believe them. Tensions remained high. *At least I'll have this on my resume*, I thought. *And the featured Arabian role looks good.* The director settled down, but one of her daughters did not.

Dancing is not for the weak. During the afternoon show, we were on stage, and the director's daughter was dancing a principal part. Everything was mapped out and staged, but she decided to take a large step back as I was due to follow her from behind. As she stepped back, she slapped me across my face and chest.

"Oops," she said under her breath.

We were on stage, so I had to keep going. We needed to finish the show. Then, when I went off stage, I saw that someone had kicked my preset. If you have a fast change—wigs, shoes, or full costumes—you will have a preset close to the curtain. You have your hairpins, tissues, or whatever you need in a tight, orderly fashion so you can run off stage and make that fast change, normally with the help of a dresser. Since my things were knocked over, I had to scramble, but I made it on stage in time for the next number.

When the show was over and we were in the locker room, a.k.a. the dressing room, I caught her up against the lockers. I got in her face, body to body, and made it clear I did not play games.

"That slap, messing up my presets . . . You would be wise not to try me again," I said.

To my shock, she yelled back, "You were flirting with my boyfriend!" She was eighteen or nineteen; I was fifteen or sixteen, and I have no idea how old the boyfriend was. He was also a dancer, and I danced one of the numbers with him. We'd all danced together in rehearsals without issues.

"You're sad," I said, "and if I wanted your boyfriend, he would be mine." Keep in mind, I had no boyfriend and didn't want one. She must have thought having a good laugh was flirting, because I always laughed and hung out with the guy dancers. Most of them complained less about dancing than the girls did.

The difference was that the boys did not need to compete with the other boys, while the girls felt they had to compete for everything. Hair, makeup, weight, dancing, leotards, shoes, parts, dance bags—every breath was a competition. As a Black dancer, my body was different, and my feet did not have a natural arch. I competed against myself, as I knew I had no room for error in my weight, the arch of my back, or my feet. One teacher duct-taped my ribs so I could not arch and told the students they could kick my feet if they saw them sickling (pointing in a weird direction). That same teacher would take a lighter and put it under the boys' behinds; if they didn't jump high enough, they would get burned.

I loved taking the boys' classes, and I was allowed to for a while. I preferred their classes, where I could jump and do power combinations, over pointe class. Unfortunately, pointe class was not optional, while the boys' class was. I was good in the boys' class—until I was told I could no longer take it. Some folks just don't want you to shine.

Once the Nutcracker season was over and I was back to my normal routine of running between dance companies and school, all I wanted to do was graduate high school and get back to New York. I had already been accepted back to Joffrey with a summer scholarship, making it my third summer there. I graduated high school, and my family threw a party for me that day. The next day, I was leaving for New York, where I would finally move into Milbank House.

Milbank House was a brownstone on 10th Street, which also happened to be down the street from Joffrey Ballet School. It only had thirty-two girls, a mix of young ladies doing all sorts of things, including a bunch of dancers, and I again had my own room. You would think there would be less drama with only thirty-two girls. That was not the case. Some guys would date their way through the house, which, of course, caused drama between the girls. Maybe it's just me, but if you know a guy has already dated three different girls in the house, and you've heard the stories and seen the fights, why would you jump in and start dating him? Trust me, he was a good-looking dude, but not enough to start messing with him. But to each their own. He was a smooth talker.

Milbank house had a curfew, and the girls really knew how to rig the bottom door to sneak in late. Of course, someone got caught and ruined it for everyone . . . until someone else was clever enough to bypass the alarm and let girls in after curfew—and get paid for it. If I planned on going out, I would stay at a friend's place. I had a few friends who lived in apartments with roommates, and there was always someone on a sofa. I only had to do the sofa a few times. Most times, I shared the bed or a blow-up mattress on the floor in my friend's room.

People were shocked when we said we had to get back home in time for curfew. It didn't stop me from hanging out in Studio 54 or Electric Lady, the recording studio on Eighth Street, with artists I will not name. They watched out for us; I was usually with my dancer friend from Iowa, and it was cute to have the ballerinas around. With all that we saw and all that was going on, they always made sure we were in good hands and got home safely. It was the '80s; when I look back now, I'm thankful those artists made sure we were not involved in the hardcore partying going on, no matter what they were doing.

My friend from Iowa was a beautiful dancer with blond hair and that wholesome look. The two of us would get dressed up on Saturday nights and go to a jazz club, where we would sip champagne or wine. We really thought we were getting away with something. The people at the jazz club knew we were underage, but they had a Black ballerina and a white ballerina sitting at the bar. We got into many places we should not have been allowed into for the same reason. We did no harm, and trust me, if we had more than two glasses of anything, that was a lot. Monday was weigh-in; we could not show up bloated.

If we did feel bloated on Sunday for any reason, we would wrap ourselves in Saran Wrap from the neck down. We would put on the plastic outfit to help us sweat, then work out and sleep in it. It worked! Was it safe? No! Did we care? No. You had a few choices as a ballerina: sweat from working out, take diet pills, take laxatives, vomit from bulimia, or not eat and be anorexic. Drugs were an option for some. I would either work out or not eat for a day or two. The rest was way too messy for me.

What I know is that living in a house where most of the girls were trying to maintain their weight meant that trying to get into the bathroom or showers was a daily struggle. Most girls had the decency to vomit in a bag they kept in their room or the toilet, but one girl would vomit in the shower and not clean it up. You learned quickly to never go into the shower or bathroom without turning the lights on, because you had no idea what you would be stepping on. That was a real part of the life of a ballet dancer, especially living with other dancers.

We lived in the heart of the West Village, just blocks from Washington Square Park, which was the center of creativity. Think New York shenanigans, drugs, chess players, dancers, artists, and musicians. Someone was always selling something legal and something not. It was fun to hang out there, but some of the girls were terrified to go through the park. They had heard all the stories of how dangerous it could be, and it was, but the energy was magic. The park, like anywhere in New York, keeps your head on swivel. For young girls thirteen and up living in a boarding house, the world was ours, and the park was our playground. We only had half of Saturday and Sunday off. We had to make the best of it.

One Saturday, we helped the son of the newly elected President of the United States ditch his Secret Service so he could hang out in the park with us. I will not mention his name. He lived across the street from the boarding house, and he was also a dancer, so it was easy to distract the Secret Service with a bunch of young dancers jumping and twirling in front of his house. We laughed for hours about how he escaped the Secret Service; they were not so happy.

As I mentioned, we had half of the day on Saturday and a full day on Sunday for time off. Sometimes, there would be extra work available, whether dancing with the main company or as an extra in commercials. At Joffrey, dancers required approval to do any extra work; our focus needed to be on class or rehearsals.

A month into the summer scholarship, I booked my first extra job for a store in Soho that wanted professional dancers to dance in the window for their new store opening. They received such great feedback that they asked if I would come back the following weekend, along with two other girls. I ended up doing that gig for a few months. While I was dancing in the window, on two separate occasions, Gregory Hines and Geoffrey Holder, passed by the window. They were two older Black stars, dancers and actors who were well respected in the industry. They each gave me the thumbs up, then came in and asked me who I was and where I danced.

Joffrey never said if I was doing well or not, but these other dancers saw something else in me. They started to speak to me about dancing beyond ballet. They said I had energy that came right through the window and onto the street. I stayed focused on and committed to my training, but I started to wonder what would happen next.

What I didn't think about was that my knees could no longer be pushed to the limit. I was close to bone on bone. As a dancer, your feet, hips, knees, and sometimes back give out. Most of my teachers had had hip surgery at some point in their careers or when they retired. It felt like a rite of passage if you were a wonderful dancer.

My knees had given me issues for as long as I could remember, and I went to orthopedic doctors from a young age. We were told that I had a childhood disease that most kids get when they grow too fast. Dancing had stunted my growth; then, when I did grow, it was rapid. And then I stopped growing. My knees didn't fare well with the type of professional training I was doing, and I was at a point where I was coming home, putting ice packs on them, and rocking back and forth from the pain. It was unbearable. It was decided: I *had* to have knee surgery.

I couldn't believe I would be out for six to eight weeks. That's a *lifetime* as a dancer, a full season of performances. I did both knees at the same time. The pain was crazy; the doctors made me sit up in the chair after surgery and start rehab on day one. I am happy I had both knees done at once. I'm not sure I would have completed the second knee otherwise.

During rehab after my knee surgery, the doctors told me I should be happy that I was walking. They said, "We don't think you will dance again."

Really, Doctor? I don't think so. I would keep dancing alright. But I made the decision that I would not be going back to Joffrey.

For one of my "extra" jobs, I worked as a promotional model for Oscar de La Renta. I wore his gowns and roamed through department stores, taking pictures and sending people to the fragrance counter. I also choreographed two off-off-Broadway shows and performed in one. It was my entry into acting. I loved the show, but I did not prepare like the other actresses. I would be backstage stretching like a dancer, not centering myself like the actresses. That was one sign acting was not for me.

After my surgery, I knew I was not finished dancing, but I did not know what was next. I saw an ad in Backstage (the Bible of all things auditions) that intrigued me, and I went to audition. I was still in rehab and should not have been thinking about auditioning for anything. My parents thought I was still in rehab in New York, and I didn't tell anyone I was going. I was now living uptown with a friend, so the boarding house couldn't tell on me whenever my parents came to visit.

I showed up to the audition for *City Lites* alongside hundreds of other girls, which was normal. The issue was that I couldn't sing! Nine out of ten times, you need to be able to sing if you want to dance on Broadway. I had once auditioned for the Broadway show *Cats*. I loved the show, and I made it all the way to the audition, where I was asked to sing. I had an audition song, *All That Jazz*! I picked that song because I could dance my way through it. Until the day they asked me to stop dancing and just sing. The directors for *Cats* pulled me aside and said, "You are a beautiful dancer, but we cannot hire you. All the roles must sing." Well, that was it for me. I knew I couldn't sing, and yes, I had taken a few lessons. It's just not one of the gifts I was given.

So, I went to the *City Lites* audition. I danced all day, and I mean *all day*. I was called back three times and made all the cuts. (If you are wondering if I was in pain, the answer is yes.) I was invited back to dance the next day, but I would also need to tap dance. *At least I don't need to sing*, I thought. Now, at any point in these pages, have you read about me tap dancing? No, because I don't tap! But I was excited to make it to day two of auditions. So, I said to myself, *Forget the knees. We can do this.*

In auditions, you typically wear something to stand out. One of my audition leotards was red—very different than the pink, baby blue, and burgundy of ballet. The choreographer called us back on stage to learn the tap number. I didn't know how to tap, but I could stay in the same direction as everyone else. I'm a performer. I know how to fake it, and I can work my face and shoulders.

On the second round of going through the steps, the choreographer said, "Girl in red! What are you doing?"

I yelled back, "I'm staying in the same direction as everyone else!" I still don't know how I was called back for the next day's audition.

The next day, I had to ice skate. This was the type of show my sister wanted me to be in. It was in Atlantic City, and it wasn't ballet. She wouldn't have to sit through another ballet or Nutcracker season. And again, if you are wondering, no, I didn't know how to ice skate. I'd never been in a skating rink or pond or touched a pair of skates.

I showed up an hour early to the skating rink. I told them I was there for the auditions and needed the skates early. I watched someone else lace up their skates and saw it was like tying pointe shoes. One of the guys I saw the day before was also there early; he couldn't skate either.

We found a little girl who was skating in circles, and I asked her, "How do I not fall?" I knew if I fell, that would be the end of my career. I wouldn't recover, because I wasn't healed yet.

The little girl looked at me and said, "Stay parallel and push off, parallel and push off."

It worked! I also realized I could do ballet arms and give face.

Other dancers started to arrive. Some of them had their own skates, while others borrowed from the counter. For once, I did not jump to be up front. We were called out on the ice by our numbers from the day before and taught a combination. I learned the combination behind the choreographer. I stayed in the same direction and threw my arms up. When in doubt, do ballet arms.

The choreographer was showing the combination, but others were watching (judging) from the sidelines. They were the people selected to move forward. When the choreographer turned around to watch us, I stopped. He said, "Why did you stop?"

"You stopped, I stopped," I said.

"Aren't you the girl in red who couldn't tap yesterday?"

"I am, but I can stay in the same direction as everyone else." (I was also the only Black girl.)

He laughed and then pulled us out individually to demonstrate our skills. My skill was trying to stay up! When he called me, he said, "OK, what can you show me?"

I did as any decent ballet dancer who just had both knees operated on does. I threw my leg up in arabesque, prayed I didn't fall, did beautiful ballet arms, and flashed a big smile.

He shook his head and said, "You are a beautiful dancer, and you have a great attitude. There will be enough time to teach you how to skate for the show."

Just like that, the audition was over. I still had not told anyone that I went to the audition. I went back to my apartment and iced my knees. A week later, I received the call that I had gotten the show. I was moving to Atlantic City.

CHAPTER 4

From Leotards to G-Strings

I waited to receive the contract, then called my parents to say, "Guess what, I'm moving to Atlantic City, and I'm dancing in a show where I also have to ice skate!"

My parents were not happy at first. They both said, "You're not supposed to be dancing. Why are you even auditioning? And you don't know how to ice skate!"

Once we moved past that, though, I needed to find a place to live in Atlantic City. I found a little studio apartment and moved in. We had only been rehearsing for a week or two when we had to take two weeks off due to a change in the casino's ownership, which left some of the dancers without a place to stay. I had one of the dancers sleeping on a lawn chair at my place, and others were in cars. It was nuts. I am not good at living with others in one space, and we were all new to each other. Some of the dancers had worked together before, but as an ensemble cast, we were new.

I was *really* the new girl, a ballet dancer from New York, used to living in my own apartment without roommates. The other dancers teased me from day one. I still had my pink ballet tights and ballet leotards, while the other girls had shorts or high-cut leotards and wore tight T-shirts tied up. It was a very different feel from my regular rehearsals. They spoke about G-strings and jazz shoes. Some danced in sneakers. Oh, and their tights had runs in them, and it was okay. In ballet, even in rehearsals, you must look presentable at all times: hair, makeup, tights without runs. I was in a new world! I was not sure about this world, but I was all in.

Rehearsals went well for me. I pick up fast, and choreographers always liked that. With the change of ownership, favorites were picked to be on the billboards and advertisements. I was a favorite with the choreographer, but not the "right look" for the new management. New experience, same issues.

I was up front in the dance numbers; then, it was time to skate. The stage would turn into an ice-skating section and then back into a stage to dance. I was not the only one who couldn't skate, so I didn't feel bad. One of the first things I had to learn was how to stop, and once I mastered stopping along with the combination, they added fans! *Lord, now we have to do the combination with fans*, I thought. We were not the skaters. We had professional skaters as the guest stars of the show, several of whom were Olympic winners. There were the people who could really skate who performed during those parts of the show, along with "dancers who can skate." I was supposed to be a "dancer who can skate."

After several months of rehearsals, the show finally opened. My parents, sister, family, and neighbors came to see the show, and my parents were shocked when they saw me on skates. They were used to the dancing and solo numbers, but that was the first time they were seeing me in a cabaret-style show. The skating with costumes, big headpieces, and fans was something else.

I was having fun with the show. I was younger than most of the girls, and my career had been different than most, so I didn't get caught up in the dressing room drama. For that, I sometimes paid the price. After the opening show, I walked into the dressing room to see that someone had written BAP (Black American Princess) across my mirror. I think the other girls thought I would get upset. I laughed and said, "True." What pissed them off was that I left it there for days and did my makeup around it.

I was dancing some of the best parts in the show, so the only thing left for me to do was improve my skating skills. I moved up from being a skater who just crossed the stage to a skater who did the next-level spins and skating combinations. I was not a leading skater, but I was out on the ice longer. I had to have my parents come back and see me perform in the new roles. They were amazed yet not surprised; they knew I would not be satisfied just being an okay skater.

I learned a lot about performing in Atlantic City. My solo numbers allowed me to show my personality. The skills I learned in ballet with quick changes came in handy performing in a show where I had over six costumes, with wig, shoe, and skate changes. It was also the first show I performed in which the show had various acts, including magicians, singers, an Argentinian Gaucho act, and animals. Can you believe one of the animal acts included a tiger that did not like the color yellow or Black people? And guess what, two of my costumes were yellow. I had to pass the tiger cage as I exited one number, because that was the act coming on as I exited. There was also a Black male dancer in the show, and we complained about how the tiger would reach out and try to grab us. I did not need to be dodging a tiger paw and doing a costume change at the same time. The performers finally agreed to keep the cage covered until we passed it. Not the best solution, but it helped.

During this show, I learned what a dance captain and a company manager do. The dance captain is responsible for keeping the show clean, overseeing rehearsals once the choreographer leaves, and being the liaison between the dancers and the company manager. I was interested in the company manager, and I would stretch in the hall in front of her office before shows. I could hear her discussions, and I would sometimes find out about things before the others. For this, the cast called me Scoop. I would give a heads-up when I knew someone important was coming to watch the show. Beyond learning the scoop, I learned how the company manager dealt with the stagehands, the owners, the backstage staff, and anything that had to do with the show. If something was off, it was her responsibility to fix it. I carry those skills I learned from her with me today.

After two years, I began to get antsy. I started going back to New York to audition for shows. One of the girls in the show also wanted to leave, so we would go to the city together. We would take the bus to the audition, then jump back on the bus to make it backstage before our call time.

On one of these trips, we signed in, got assigned a number, then were called in by number and taught a combination, as is normal in auditions. My friend and I were in the same group, but she was cut before she could dance. The directors said, "thank you" and dismissed her immediately because they did a body casting. That means you must fit the body type they are looking for before you get to dance one step! I was asked to stay. When that happens, you wait until all the numbers are called, and then you start again. They kept me on for four rounds, and time was running out to make the bus back to Atlantic City. My friend was not pleased. She had been cut before she could really dance, and she waited all day—and I mean *all day*—just for me to get cut too. After that, I started going into the city on my own.

During that time, I saw an audition listing for a show on one of the Caribbean Islands. I had always wanted to travel. I thought if I could travel and dance, that would be wonderful. I had several callbacks, and I got the gig even though they knew I could not sing.

I now had to figure out the rehearsal schedule so I could travel back and forth between Atlantic City and New York, and back to Atlantic City in time to do the show. I had been in rehearsals for the new show for a week when I decided that I needed to give notice—first to the show in Atlantic City that I would be leaving, then to my landlord.

I went to the company manager and gave my two-week notice. I said I could stay an extra week if she needed me to, and she asked me to do so. When I went into the city for my next rehearsal, I noticed there was a Black girl in the corner who tried to move whenever I moved. The next day, the same thing.

The director pulled me to the side and told me, "We are sorry, the producer's girlfriend's show is closing. She needs a job, and she can sing, so we have to let you go." (You know the golden rule: one Black girl per show. It was rare to ever have more than one.)

I headed back to Atlantic City, thinking, *Now what?* I had given notice, but I knew I could stay longer in the apartment. *What will I do for work?* I knew I didn't want to stay in the show.

The next day, I told a few people that I would not be doing the Caribbean show. Because news travels like lightning backstage, most of the cast kept telling me to go speak to the company manager about staying. I had not been replaced yet. But something kept telling me I would be okay. The manager did come to ask if I wanted to stay, but I said no. I stayed an extra month because one of the girls became ill, and they would have been short two girls. It gave me time to decide what was next.

What was next: *I'm moving to Las Vegas!*

When I announced that I was moving to Vegas, people laughed. "You do know you're short, and Black, right?" they said. Very few shows, if any, took short dancers, and never Black dancers. Not the main shows on the strip. Smaller shows, yes, but very few of the big-name shows had Black dancers, male or female.

I reached out to one of the girls I was friendly with who was working in Vegas in a mid-size show. She was shorter than me, Puerto Rican, and a beautiful dancer. She told me she was going to be leaving to tour with one of the Argentinian Gaucho acts, so I could come to stay in her apartment while she was in town and after she left. *Perfect.* I packed my stuff and headed to Vegas in August with my ice skates over my shoulder. The sister show, *City Lites,* was still open, and in the worst case, I figured maybe I'd audition there.

I arrived in Vegas with a temporary place to stay and no car, but with the foresight to find out where the auditions were being held. My friend connected me with a girl who had just moved to Las Vegas. She had the car, I had gas money and the audition list, and off we went.

JJ and I became tight, and we went to many auditions together. In between, I worked as a model (my fallback job) and an extra in a few movies. I somehow connected with a production crew and began hanging out with them, learning new production tools and skills that I had no idea I would use in the future. I had been in Las Vegas for three months with no work when, in one day, both JJ and I received two job offers, one for GLOW (Gorgeous Ladies of Wrestling—it was a thing back then) and another for Minsky's Burlesque.

I went to a GLOW training and couldn't stop laughing on the first day. Jumping off the ring into the center of the mat, slamming my hands down, and grunting was not going to be for me. I left the rehearsal, called them back, and declined the offer.

If I thought *City Lites* in Atlantic City was far from ballet, Minsky's Burlesque was a whole new world. The show was a revival of old vaudeville performers and burlesque shows. I had feathers in Atlantic City; in Vegas, I had no top—but lots of feathers and rhinestones. It was my first topless show. *I'm in Vegas, baby*!

The point of the show was that there was a type of woman for everyone—tall, short, dark, light, blonde. Myself included, there were exactly three Black female dancers in the show. The show was unique in its casting, and there were different featured roles for burlesque performers. I decided to audition for Sally Rand. Sally Rand was white, but they wanted the role to be on pointe, and since I was a classical ballet dancer, I was set on auditioning for the role. The funny thing was, there was a tall white girl there who was also a ballet dancer. I knew I would not get the part, but I wasn't going to just hand it to her. After our little competition for the role, which she was awarded, we became friends. We are still close friends to this day.

During rehearsals, the producers brought in retired but famous burlesque dancers to teach us the stripper's dip and other tricks with fans. One of the other Black dancers in the cast portrayed the one Black burlesque role, and the understudy was not me but the other Black dancer. Why, you ask, if I was supposed to be such a good dancer? Well, for that role, you had to twirl the tassels on your breasts, and I had very little to twirl them with. But I wasn't sad about missing out on that role; I had featured spots throughout the show.

I was hired as a dancer, not a showgirl. Still, it was made clear that even the dancers would be topless in a portion of the opening and closing. The dancers opened the show in full costume and performed a dance number, then the showgirls came out after us. They were taller, topless, and did less dancing, but with more ornate costumes. Once the showgirls finished, the dancers returned to the stage topless to finish out the big opening. I thought it would bother me more than it did, but it didn't—until my parents came to watch.

I remember saying, "Wait, my dad's out there!"

The other girls just yelled, "Who cares? Go!"

You may be shocked to learn that Vegas does not run on people's warm hearts. It's a transient town. While I was performing there, many dancers came and went. Everyone knew someone working a show on stage, backstage, or in the band. Performers knew performers.

During rehearsals, people would break off into their little cliques. It happens. Ballet, Broadway, theater—it is what it is. Minsky's Burlesque was all about who was and wasn't in the "cool girl dressing room." My friend NNA and I were in Dressing

Room 1, the "cool girl" dressing room. Three other dressing rooms were labeled "not as cool." It's important to note that the true stars of the show enjoyed private dressing rooms, and at the heart of it all was Bambi Jr., the star. With a legacy steeped in glamour, she's the daughter of a famous burlesque dancer whose name still echoes through the industry. Following in her mother's footsteps, Bambi Jr. embodies the same beauty, charisma, and allure that made her mother a legend. As always, I hung out with whomever I liked, speaking and joking with everyone.

The show wasn't difficult, and we performed it twice a night. During our break between shows, something was always going on. One girl would be in a fight with her boyfriend or husband, and another would be leaving to meet her boyfriend in a different show across town, hoping to make it back in time for our second show. One of the girls used to gamble like crazy; one would drink a bit too much, but not enough to get caught . . . until she did. There was always some type of shenanigans going on. Everyone was enjoying life.

It was the mid-'80s, and the men, a.k.a. groupies of the show, always wanted the dancers to hang out with them. Some of the men paid for everything, including rent, hair, lashes, and whatever the girl wanted, so that they could be around a group of dancers. When I found out what some of the ladies were doing, I thought, *If that's what you want to do for cash or to party, who am I to judge?* I knew I would distance myself from them, though. Granted, some of the men were decent, but some made my skin crawl.

There was a famous vaudeville act featuring two men in their eighties, and they began inviting some of the girls out. The girls were hand-picked, not only from the "cool dressing room." I began to hear about some of the things that were going on at night because the girls would gossip and brag about it before the show.

I was coming down the stairs before a show one night when one of the men from the vaudeville act pulled me aside. "Leslie, you know why you aren't being invited out when that one group of men comes to town, right?" he asked.

"It's not my thing," I said.

"And you are not that type of girl," he said. "You are very different from the other girls; you don't need any of this. This is not your last stop, just a stop to say you did it. Please stay as you are."

The girls in the "cool room" started not seeming so cool to me. I begin doing other gigs outside of the show—smaller dance shows after my show, or work on films—so I didn't hang out much with the others. I was labeled "stuck-up" because I wanted to do more than what was in front of me. The man was right; being in the show was not the end for me. It was just the beginning.

Call me the stuck-up goody two-shoes if you want, but when trouble calls, I'm the first place people run. If you come to me, you know I'm going to give it to you straight. I've helped friends out of abusive relationships by devising plans for them to escape and helped others get into rehab. The few times girls got into trouble or were too drunk to drive, they would call me or find their way to my door. They knew that for one, I would keep their secret, two, I would take them in, and three, I would tell them if it was a pattern. One of the girls was dating a cop. Instead of taking the girls in when they were stopped for drunk driving one night, he brought them all to my place. He said, "If you don't take them, I have to take them in." The following day was a rude awakening for the girl who was driving when she awoke on my floor and saw my face.

I had my fair share of fun and madness in Vegas, but I keep what I did private. I will tell you, Vegas is not for the weak; it is easy to get sucked in. I decided to do what I do best: work and learn. I became friends with the stagehands on my shows. I felt it was important to understand everyone's jobs, which allowed me to do what I did on stage. One of the guys came from a family of electricians and stagehands. I mentioned how much I loved what was going on behind the stage as much as I loved being on the stage (well, maybe not as much), and I started hanging out with him between shows. He began showing me different things about pulling the ropes, designing lighting, and calling the lights. After we spent a lot of time together, he got me into the electrician union so I could take a few classes and eventually be called to work a few of the big events in town.

On Wednesdays, I had my night off from the show, and one Wednesday morning, I received a call asking if I could come in and work the crew for a large event. I called a friend, one of the guys in the band, and said, "I need a tool belt to work as part of the crew for tonight's big event. I don't have tools—or a belt!"

Bless him. He said, "I'll bring some tools, and I'll take you to get a tool belt."

We went to Home Depot, where I picked up the additional tools and a belt, and I showed up to the event with my new gear.

The head guy looked at me, probably wondering how I had gotten there and why. He shook his head and sent me to a section where the second guy was no more thrilled to see me than the first. But I was proud to be a part of the crew. I think I was the only Black female there, and I was a dancer, so I didn't look like I had the muscles to lift anything. I was assigned to roll the cables, which meant I had to keep the roll moving as the cables were laid out. They were heavy, but I lifted them and kept up with the guy I was assigned to work with. At the end of the night, he was impressed. "I didn't have much hope for you," he said, "but you kept up. See you around."

I learned so much that night about production by just keeping my mouth closed and paying attention—not only to what I needed to do, but also to how others were moving. At the end of the night, when the event was set up, I had a chance to look up, and I kept thinking about what an experience I had just been given. I was tired but excited. I had no idea if I would ever use what I learned, but it felt thrilling to learn it.

CHAPTER 5

Cruising

A little over a year after moving there, I wasn't as enamored with living in Vegas anymore. I wanted to travel. I had heard dancers talk about cruise ships and smaller shows abroad, and then I saw an audition for a cruise ship. I had learned that there were two ships that dancers wanted to work for; this audition was for one of them. The ship had a high-end clientele. There was only one dinner seating, and dancers only hosted a dinner table and one activity per two-week cruise. I wouldn't have to work other jobs besides dancing. The shows and costumes were supposed to be amazing, and the choreographer was well known.

I auditioned, and I got the gig! I gave notice to Minsky's that I was leaving; since they were down a few girls, they asked if I would stay during rehearsals. I agreed because that meant rehearsal pay *plus* full pay from the Minsky's show. During rehearsals for the ship, the choreographer mentioned she had a few open roles. I told my friend NNA about it, and she got the gig on a different ship.

I was part of the swing crew. We would change ships every two months, which meant I would see the world faster than most. Dancers worked on the ship for six months, then had two months off. During the months of rehearsal, I was made dance captain, which meant I would get paid more, and more importantly, I got my own cabin! It also meant I would be the liaison between the ship, dancers, and company on land. I had to keep the costumes organized, the show clean, and the dancers rehearsed.

I finally left the show in Vegas so I could focus on what I needed to pack for six months in different climates. The choreographers kept saying, "Don't bring what you can't carry."

I thought, *How am I expected to pack ball gowns, coats, casual, summer and winter outfits, plus hair products, and carry it all?* At least all the dance stuff, except personal dance items, got packed with the costumes. Still, it was a lot! If you know me, you know I love fashion. I was so lucky I didn't need to share a cabin.

It was spring, and we were preparing to leave when the choreographer gathered us for the team meeting. She shared the expectations: the one big rule was to never sit on a bar stool, and to always give guests the open seat, no matter how much they insisted you take it. Let the older women dance with the men. There were drinking rules, weight rules. Needless to say, the weight rules on a ship are as bad as the ballet weight rules, and yes, a few girls and one guy were let go because of weight. On a ship, there's food and drinks everywhere, so you have to watch it.

We got to a point in the meeting where she began to talk about my presence on the team. "Leslie is the first Black person who has been allowed on any of the ships, as an employee and as a dancer," she said. "Please know that some guests may ask why she has been allowed to dance with you or why she is in charge. It is because she is a brilliant dancer. I selected her to be the dance captain because she can handle the business side, as well as dance. End of conversation."

It didn't faze me at the time. I was used to being the first.

As dancers, we had wonderful working conditions. We slept in passenger cabins, with two dancers to a cabin; we ate in the dining room with the guests, except for on show nights. We wore uniforms during the day and dressed for the theme of the night along with passengers, unless we were performing.

You may be wondering if it was a big deal that I was the first Black dancer or employee on the ship, and if that special permission to join the show was necessary. The short answer is, "yes and no." The crew was surprised but fantastic. Most of the crew was from Scandinavia, Europe, or the Philippines. The ship was Norwegian, and the senior-level staff were all Norwegian or from that region. To the Italians, I was their little chocolate drop. Each group took me in in its own way.

I'm sure there were whispers about the Black dancer. After the show, I would receive praise and then the "How did you come to dance on the ship?" questions. On occasion, I would receive a side-eye. Though I was the first Black dancer there, I hoped I would not be the last. It's funny how people never questioned my talent, but my color. I couldn't get hung up on their questions, though. I had come on the ship to dance and see the world.

I left with my first group of dancers to join the cruise, thinking I would switch ships as planned in two months. But then I received a call asking me to stay on the ship for an additional six months. The previous dance captain would not be returning, and they felt they needed someone strong to handle that cast. My heart sank. As much as I didn't want to pack up my bags, I had been excited about the itinerary for the swing crew. I agreed to stay, and guess what: NNA was on the same crew! I danced many of the parts that NNA danced and had her costumes altered for me. (She is three inches taller than I am, even though I like to say we are the same height.) Her ship was the first ship I joined as the swing crew, which meant we had to alter costumes to fit the dancers on board.

The group really liked the dance captain who left; she was easy. I was not easy. If it is my responsibility to keep a show clean, we will rehearse until it is. The other girl was not tight on paperwork since she didn't want to tell on anyone, while I did my reports as they were meant to be. I told them, "I can only keep your drinking and lack of singing talent a secret for so long before the guests start complaining." If they didn't work on it, I made it clear they would need to be replaced. I also couldn't keep their weight gains a secret; it shows. "If I get a call and I'm asked to weigh someone before the scheduled weigh-in, it's not a good look for either of us," I warned. As dance captain, I was always balancing being a performer and wanting to hang out with the cast with being the one who must be responsible, accountable to the people making the big decisions. Who knew being dance captain would prepare me for a business career.

One night during a formal dinner, I heard one of the dancers' voices rise. You may know this story if you read my first book. I was surprised, as this was one of the quieter dancers who more or less played by the rules. Keep in mind, I was asked to stay on the ship because the dancers in this group were something else!

Ted was not usually the guy to get loud. When I turned to see what was happening at the table, I saw him storming out of the dining room, which meant I now needed to know what had happened.

Ted was pissed. "The guest kept asking why you were on the ship and why you were in charge of us," he said. The big issue had finally exploded: *Why was I there?*

I looked at Ted and stated, "You do not need to fight for me. It's about him, not me or you. I'm staying here; he gets off in a week. If he comes back in the next four months, he will have to see me again." I was and am used to the "Why are you here?" questions, as well as the "I'm surprised you are here" or "I've never seen you here before" comments.

Ted reminded me that his group had not received the talk about me being the first, because they were not my original group. He calmed down, but he always watched out for others. Even today, Ted stands up for people when he feels there is an injustice.

Other than that incident, life on the cruise ship was interesting. I was treated like a queen by the staff and most passengers. I was invited to join off-ship excursions and lavished with jewelry and gifts. The dancers and I had somewhat gotten into a rhythm.

NNA and I decided that, because we were close friends, we would not hang out. That way, there wouldn't be any favoritism; also, we knew we would be trouble together. The funny part was, she was dating someone on the officers' deck, and so was I. We weren't supposed to be on that deck, and we tried to keep things low-key. (There weren't rules about dating, just about who was allowed on that floor.) But let's be real, nothing stays quiet on a ship! If it seems there are no issues, that meant everyone is simply keeping it on the low.

One morning, we had an early call, and we decided to slowly creep off the officers' deck back to our rooms in time for rehearsals. I peeked my head out and saw NNA's blond hair poking out, then two other dancers' heads. "On the count of three, run!" I said. "I see nothing, just be on stage on time." We all made it. If you were looking for missing dancers on that ship, you would always want to check the officers' deck first.

A few things happened on the ship that I would question today. Ted digitized one of the shows we performed together, a compilation of old Broadway shows and musicals. Looking at the costumes today, you could not pay me enough to wear several of them, and there was one number that I would never perform today. When I flipped up the skirt on the costume, it was a Black mammy from *Gone with the Wind*. Yes, I wore the costume and flipped it so the mammy could glow in the dark. Even then, I wasn't happy, but it was part of "art and a musical." Today, I'd say "Art be damned."

I recall how the show opened with me sticking my head out from behind the side curtain, singing (lip syncing), "I'm a country girl from head to toe." I laughed because I loved the looks on the audience's faces when I was the first one out for that number. But when I look back at the show, my heart sinks. Yes, I was the first Black dancer on the ship. Victory count one. Victory count two, I had no major issues with colleagues or guests. Performing racist numbers, or numbers with racist undertones? No victory there.

That mammy number that turns my stomach today was not a glaring issue at the time, though. At the time, the glaring issue I fixated on was simply getting myself on the ship. Lesson learned: There can be more than one glaring issue. It still makes my heart sink to look back at it. I cried when I later watched that number.

Proud of the dancer and sad for the dancer, all in one show.

I finished my nine months with the ship. When it was finally time for me to get off, I told them never to do that to someone again. It was too much. But I also saw and experienced amazing things while on the ship, which solidified my desire to dance and travel. I saw Alaska, the Caribbean Islands, Canada, the Panama Canal, Colombia, Brazil—so many beautiful places. Being on a ship for nine months is no joke. For the Black girls and women wondering what I did about my hair? There was a beauty salon on the ship, and the girls from London were versed in different hair textures. One in particular would wash, relax, and trim my hair for me. The hair problem on the ship was solved! I always traveled with my own products too.

Working on a cruise ship is also one of the best ways to learn about other cultures. It helped that, as dancers, we could get off at each port. We wouldn't have shows on those nights, which allowed us to explore cities and countries on repeat. If we wanted, we could dive into learning where we were. I loved it. I'll never forget the time we disembarked in Rio de Janeiro, Brazil, and woke up to watch the sunrise over Christ the Redeemer's statue. It is still one of the most beautiful sights I have ever seen.

By the time I left, I was ready to get off the ship, but it was still bittersweet. I decided to go back to Las Vegas, where I figured I'd find something. I found out my apartment would not be ready until two weeks after my arrival. I made the best of it by checking which auditions were available, and I went back to Minsky's to see the show. While there, I ran into one of the executive's sons, whom I was friendly with when I worked in the show.

"Leslie, what are you up to now?"

"Looking for the next gig and waiting to move into my apartment," I replied.

He looked at me and said, "I'll let you stay here at the hotel for free if you come back and dance in the show for a few weeks."

I was shocked, but that was a great deal. I wouldn't need to pay for a hotel, I already knew the show, and I could work while looking for the next gig. I could not have asked for a better arrangement.

It didn't take long to find the next gig.

I had only been in Vegas for a few weeks when I ran into the Argentinian Gaucho act that appeared in the Atlantic City show; they were heading to Curacao. They hired me as lead dancer and dance captain, and I was off. The contract was great: six days a week, one show a night. We lived at the resort, and we had a food and drink allowance. It was a beautiful island, and we performed a fabulous one-and-a-half-hour show.

When people say "island time," they mean it. Things did not move fast! I didn't do much but read during the day. My mom came out to visit, which must have been when I spent the longest time out of my room during the day—unless I was going to buy a Baby Ruth candy bar from the gift shop. I did become friends with one of the women at the resort, and on her day off, we would go to lunch or hang out. She was surprised to see a Black American dancer in one of the shows. She introduced me to her friends, who were studying international business, as well as her family, and I enjoyed meeting people beyond the resort.

Three months later, it was time to return to Vegas. I began thinking of Vegas as a holding pad. I would do a gig, come back to Vegas, work a little bit, find the next gig that would take me out of the country, rinse, and repeat. I connected with my apartment's management, so I'd call in advance and tell them which day I would return, and after that first issue, I always had a furnished place ready when I got back.

I worked a few shows as a swing dancer, so I was working two or three different shows during the week. So much for "You will never work in Vegas!" Once you are in the circle, you let folks know when you are returning and see who bites. After Curacao, I stayed three months, then went to Aruba with the same Gaucho act. The show was bigger. I had two more solos, and we planned to stay there for five months. Instead of letting my apartment go, I sublet it to a friend.

Aruba was beautiful. At the time, it was still under Dutch control. They used to call me a bat because I would only come out at night there. The sun is hot, and I do not need a tan. On our day off, the Gaucho act (which consists of two brothers, by the way) would jump on a friend's private plane with a few of the dancers and head to Argentina. We would leave early in the morning so we could have the full day and fly back in the early afternoon, in time for the show the next day.

On one of the trips, I sat next to the pilot, asking questions. He looked at me and said, "I'll do the pedals, you focus on the direction."

I thought he was joking and turned the plane a bit too fast.

"Do not let her fly the plane," the others screamed. "Do not let her con you into letting her fly the plane!"

Oops, my bad, I thought, still steering.

When you become friends with people outside of the dance world, whether traveling or staying home, you get to experience life through others' eyes. While in Aruba, I received many invitations to go sailing, boating, or to dinners hosted at government officials' homes or with the local celebrity. As the only Black American girl in the show, I was a bit of a local celebrity myself.

After the show in Aruba, I did what I usually did and went back to Vegas. While I was collecting my luggage after landing, a woman swung her bag into my foot, and I ended up with a hairline fracture. (Because of this incident, I detest grabbing my bags at the airport to this day! I will always try to find the most out-of-the-way place to take my bag off the carousel.) With that, I was back in Vegas with no gig and a semi-broken foot. I wasn't in a cast, but it was still not a good look.

Soon after arriving, I got a call from a choreographer that I had worked with in the past. "What are you doing now?" he asked.

"I'm just getting back into town," I said.

"Why didn't you call me in advance?" he shouted. "I just cast the James Brown Tour and offered the last spot to someone yesterday." He told me to meet him at a hotel where he was doing a final casting for a show going to Greece.

This is perfect, I thought. I haven't had to audition for the last few years, and I'm now receiving the calls. It's an artist's dream, getting the call to come do what you do.

I jumped in a taxi, crutches and all. I unwrapped my foot and left my crutches in the hall before going in to meet with the choreographer. He told me that it would be at least a month before rehearsals began. *Thank God, my foot can heal.*

"I'm sorry, I offered the lead to a dancer already," he said. "I also offered dance captain to someone." But he told me he would create featured dance roles for me.

I thought, *I don't need to be the lead if I'm being featured, and who needs the headache of dance captain?* I just wanted to go to Athens.

I signed the contract on the spot. I would leave for Athens in two to three months. I told my parents I wanted to keep the apartment. I would sublease again because the contract was only six months, and then I'd be back. They would keep an eye on everything, periodically checking in from New Jersey.

Before leaving for Greece, the crew was invited to a show starring Ben Vereen, a well-respected actor, dancer, and Broadway Star. We were invited backstage, where he shared stories of the theater and reminded us that we needed to stick together while traveling abroad. How many times did we bring up his name amidst the madness within the first few weeks of our arrival in Greece? Sticking together was already proving to be shaky.

CHAPTER 6

The Spirit of Europe

We arrived in Greece on a beautiful early fall day. We had packed our ball gowns and formal attire, as we needed to be dressed to go to the theater each night. The Rex Theater was reopening with the biggest celebrity Greek singers, specialty acts, and, for the first time, American dancers.

Sounds amazing. Rightfully so, you would think we would have been in a decent hotel. Instead, the organizers dropped us off at a somewhat shady-looking hotel and gave us our room assignments. I was rooming with an easygoing dancer who kept to herself, so I was happy about that. But then we opened the door to find a classic, older European style setup with a shower as part of the bedroom and water running under the bed. The beds were twin beds; the sheets and spread looked worn. *This is* not *going to do*, I thought.

I connected with the other Black dancer in the show, and we searched for the dance captain. "These conditions are unacceptable," we told her.

"It's fine," was all she had to say.

"No love, it's *not* fine. Where is the choreographer?"

The other dancers were not happy, either. The lead dancer and I both had credit cards and began looking for alternative hotels. While all of this was going on, the man who worked for the Big Boss at the theater and spoke English came back to the hotel. I began to explain that there was no way I would be living in these conditions, coming out in ballgowns and dancing a three-hour show for six months. We would be leaving that night for a different hotel, and we would leave Greece the next day, or whenever we could book a flight out.

He was stunned. He must have been thinking, one, *Why are these girls speaking to me like this?* And two, *They're dancers; you get what you get.* He told us the English dancers lived there. But we were American dancers, and we had different standards. The choreographer was called back, and we spoke with him. Meanwhile, the dance captain, who was supposed to stand up for us, did nothing.

The choreographer pulled me and the lead dancer aside and begged us to stay the night. "It's been a long day," he said. "Let's work it out in the morning."

Because of him, we settled down and settled the dancers. "Once we get to the theater tomorrow, it will need to be addressed," we agreed. I told everyone not to unpack.

They picked us up the next day. I was still hot, the lead dancer was hot, and the other dancers were just waiting to see what was going to happen. The dance captain was still clueless. We began to block out the show on the stage and did a light rehearsal for the choreography before beginning a full rehearsal. We had learned the show in Vegas, and now we needed to make it ours in the space.

When we took a break, the same gentleman who had spoken with us the night before, the one who worked for the Big Boss (aka the owner of the theater), whispered something to the choreographer. I took the opportunity to ask if the hotel situation was being addressed. At first, he ignored me; I knew it wasn't a language barrier, because he spoke English! I asked again, and he half answered.

We were called back to the stage, but I was extra hot now, and so was the lead dancer. I declared that we needed a meeting. Keep in mind, I was not the dance captain, who had decided she didn't want to cause problems on the first day. I ignored her. The next break, I looked at the choreographer and said, "If we don't have a meeting with them, I'm done."

Meanwhile, in the shadow of the theater, (which, by the way, was still being built) was a man who looked like Papa Smurf. He was speaking fast and furious to the man from the night before. The meeting got called, and he looked at us as if we had lost our minds. Women don't speak up and out like that. Plus, didn't we know he owned the place and was very powerful in Greece?

The man who spoke English introduced the theater owner to the group, and he went on and on about the history of the theater and why it was important to him. All I heard was Charlie Brown's teacher: "Whaa, whaa, whaa . . ."

I chimed in. "If it is this important to you, then the living conditions of your performers for the next six months should also be important to you."

He said something in Greek and looked at me.

I looked at the man who spoke English. Granted, not one dancer had spoken up, even though everyone had had something to say before they found out he was the Big Boss.

"The hotel is unacceptable," I said, and was again told that the English dancers stayed there. "That's on them. We are American, and the hotel is not up to the standards you should want for your theater." I asked for my words to be translated as I said them.

The boss looked at the other dancer speaking up along with me; it was the two Black girls who happened to be the lead and the featured dancers of the show. "Give me until the afternoon," he said.

We went back to rehearsal. That afternoon, the Big Boss came back and told the choreographer to take a break in the middle of a number. He asked for me, the lead dancer, and the choreographer to come with him. We went, of course, along with the man who spoke English. The other dancers just stood there, thinking we were about to get fired. I knew a few girls would have been happy, imagining they could dance our roles. Instead, we walked to the hotel next door and looked at the rooms. We came back to tell everyone we would be moving in the morning.

If the other dancer and I had not spoken up, we would have spent six months in Greece in a horrible hotel listening to everyone complain. If you want something, say something!

Later that week, we were in full rehearsal costumes and lights when, all of a sudden, an older man with a tray of tea stepped on stage and said, "Tea for Ms. Leslie!"

I looked around thinking, *This a joke.*

Rehearsal had to come to a full stop because the Big Boss felt I should have a tea break. I don't need to tell you how the other dancers felt. It turned out the Big Boss liked that I stood up for myself and others; he had not seen that before. He thought I was a beautiful dancer, and he wanted to make sure I enjoyed my time in Greece. Trust me, I did!

A week after the show opened, I became the dance captain. Not because of the hotel situation, although it was a factor. We had been told not to travel on our first weekend off, but don't you know, the dance captain—the one who was supposed to make sure we knew and followed the rules—went and traveled to an island and got stuck. She barely made it back to the show for the opening number. The Big Boss was not happy with her. The choreographer was furious too, and the rest of the dancers didn't have much respect for her. The bosses pulled me in and asked if I wanted to be dance captain. Along with that came my own hotel room and extra money. Of course, I said yes.

Greece was good to me. My mom came to visit, and we ran around visiting islands and sightseeing. My friends from Aruba came and surprised me on stage for New Year's Eve. I modeled for several advertisements and shot an ice cream commercial. Greece had a hot modeling scene. The Big Boss held true to his promise. We became friends, hung out, and toured the country when I wasn't dancing, and I had opportunities the other dancers did not have. We had a special relationship that came in handy when I chipped my tooth and needed a dentist, or when one of the dancers busted his knee and needed surgery.

While living in Greece, I met a photographer from Vienna, Austria. I flew over to visit during one of our breaks and met another American dancer, as well as a few other folks who told me I should come there next.

I returned to Greece to finish my contract. The Big Boss asked me to extend it, even proposing to move me into an apartment. It was tempting, but I needed to move on.

Let's see what Vienna will do.

Vienna started off a bit weird. My one friend, who was a dancer, knew a guy who had a place he rented from a friend. She was Austrian, and he was from Suriname. The apartment was beautiful, with a marble staircase in the entryway, two huge bedrooms, lots of space, and a decent kitchen (I don't cook, so no big deal). The toilet was its own room, and the shower was next to the kitchen. *Strange, but okay.* I was going to live in Europe. Only one issue: the guy and I didn't like each other. He needed the money, and I needed a place to stay, so we made a deal. I rarely saw him. He was a makeup artist and was always off and about.

It was my first time living in Europe with no dance job and my first time renting an apartment in Europe, and I didn't have any of the free food at restaurants or bars that I usually had when performing in a show. I needed to figure it out, and I did not speak the language. I had two other friends in town. I went to dance classes and met other dancers. I signed with a modeling agency, which was why I had moved to Vienna. But I was only with the agency for two months before I left because they treated us like small children. I got it: The girls were young. But I could handle my life and didn't feel like I needed to check in for every little thing. *Just tell me what job I've booked and where I need to be, and I'll find my way.*

Without the agency, I booked very interesting modeling jobs. I was on the jumbotron in the middle of town. I modeled for ski catalogs. I was in a video for the hottest rock band, and that video played everywhere. I started dating the lead singer, so we were all around town. I also went on tour, as I performed with them and choreographed their music video. I was cast as the lead for a commercial for Vienna's version of Tide laundry detergent; it was a big commercial and played in movie theaters, as well as on TV.

I had become friendly with my roommate by this time, and he hooked me up with jobs. I also started teaching dance as a guest teacher. Dance is universal; in every language, we just need to count to eight. I taught adult jazz and ballet classes, which was fun. I was not making a lot of money, but I wanted to live on my own without help from my parents' credit card. I did have to break down and charge a winter coat, though. It was cold in Vienna! My roommate and I barely scraped the money together to afford coal for the heater. We had several cold days and nights. Luckily, he cooked. He made an amazing dish with dried shrimp and noodles from his home country, and it became my favorite. The bread in Vienna was fantastic—a bit too fantastic. I was figuring it out.

There were not many Black girls walking down the streets when I was living in Vienna. I wasn't surprised people stared, but they did more than that. They refused to help with directions, especially the older folks. Some people, young and old, would not sit next to me on the train. I would sit down, and they would get up and move. That didn't bother me. And it didn't bother me when the older woman who lived on the floor above us asked if she could touch my skin. She was around eighty years old, and she said, "I know times are changing, and so should I with the time I have left." I took her hand, and we walked up the marble staircase. She looked at me and thanked me in her broken English. I wasn't upset—I saw kindness in her eyes.

I am not, and I have never been, a big letter writer. But one day I wrote a letter to my parents and went to the post office a few blocks from the apartment. There was a construction site next door to the post office, and the men who were working on the scaffolding yelled "Nigga" at me. I knew the difference between negro (Black) and nigga. I was called a nigga, followed by peals of laughter.

My heart stopped, but my feet did not. I pulled my head up, looked at them, went into the post office, and mailed my letter. Now I had a choice to make: Take a different direction back to the house so I wouldn't have to pass them or walk out with my head up and go home. They yelled it again as I walked by. I prayed they didn't throw anything at me since my back was turned. I was clear that little girls and boys once had water hoses and dogs turned on them when they tried to go to school, and that they'd fought to walk and sit and just *be* in public places. But it was the late '80s, and I would not let anyone come at me with their nonsense.

I decided that if I was the first "nigga" they had seen, they would see me every day. I started to write a letter or postcard to friends or family every day, and I walked back and forth to the post office for close to two weeks. The workers finally left me alone. I guess they thought I was a *crazy* nigga. My mother begged me to be careful, but she knew I would not back down.

I had one other incident in Vienna when I was coming home from a show rehearsal on the train. One of the dancers had told me, "If you don't have a ticket, don't worry. You can buy one on the train." I saw the train coming, ran to jump on it, and sat down. When the ticket agent came over, he was already annoyed just by my being there. He shouted for the ticket.

I said, "yes" and went to hand him the money. He started yelling as I sat there and asked, "I buy the ticket from you?"

"No English!" he bellowed.

"Okay, ticket," I said, and shoved the money toward him.

That didn't go well. The other ticket agent joined him, and now I was boxed in. I just kept repeating, "I'll buy a ticket. Here is money."

The ticket agent started yelling something like, "American, negro . . ."

A younger guy stood up and told them to stop. He would pay for me, and they could punch his card twice.

The agents said no, and I couldn't believe it when a few others stood up and made them leave me alone. The young people spoke English and told me to always buy my ticket before getting on the train. Lesson learned.

I lived in Vienna for nine months. The highlight was when my nephew was born—on my birthday. I had been wondering why my family had not called that day. I was shooting a TV commercial and was gone from early morning until late into the evening. (No cell phones at that time.) When I arrived back at the apartment, there was a message waiting on my answering machine: "Happy Birthday! And guess who else was just born on your birthday?"

My family thought I might not want to share a birthday. It's just my sister and me, and I'm the youngest. But I could not have been happier. I never saw my sister pregnant, since I was living overseas, and I only saw her get married because I received permission to get off the ship and go home while we were dry-docked. I flew in the night before the wedding, fitted my dress, and was gone the day after. So, it was extra special to have a connection with my nephew that I didn't get in advance. From the day he was born and every day since, he has brought me joy. He is bright and gifted—and my birthday mate.

Although I have no desire to return to Vienna, it was an experience for my first time living in Europe. When I think about Vienna, one memory always comes back to me. HIV and AIDS were becoming very scary, and I saw many male dancers become sick. Some would disappear, as they would go back to their country, or they would pass away because they were rejected by their families and had no money for meds. My friend became ill, and he had good days and bad days.

I would go to the hospital's AIDS ward to visit him sometimes. During one visit, I ran into another dancer I knew. He was surprised and scared to see me there and begged me to keep his secret. I also started visiting a different dancer whom I'd worked with at the same hospital. I was not scared to catch the disease, as I followed the precautions the nurse shared. I couldn't imagine being sick and knowing you may die while you're alone in a foreign country. I went to visit; I held the pan for him to vomit. I watched over my other friend, and I kept my promise to the other dancer.

Later, I received a postcard from the dancer who had asked me to keep his secret, thanking me. He was very ill, but he wanted me to know what it meant to him to see me pop in and never expose him. I visited my other friend until he passed. His parents came to visit; they were older and very confused. I tried to comfort them by telling them how amazing a dancer he was and how happy I was to have him as a dance partner and friend. I wanted them to know he was much more than a gay man, and that he was loved by others.

My other friend, whom I originally went to visit, was in and out of the hospital. It was when he was going through a good time, and we were all celebrating the cocktail of meds finally doing their thing, that his boyfriend came home and found him hanging in the closet. What we thought was a good moment was clearly still a dark time for him. I learned from his death to never assume someone is in a good space when they are going through something, but to ask and continue to be there.

I still find myself thinking about him—and how deeply his death changed me. There's a saying: "Check on your strong friends." I often wonder how one lives with the weight of finding someone they love lost to suicide, as I lost touch with my friend's boyfriend soon after his death. The image of my friend lingers quietly in my mind. But more powerful than the pain is the memory of his kindness, which continues to live in my heart.

After nine months, my time in Vienna was slowly winding down. The rock star lead singer and his band were on tour performing at summer festivals. I went with them to dance to their popular song, for which I had starred in the video. After the tour, I was invited to teach as a guest dance teacher in Denmark. I was excited, because Denmark was on my list. I spent two weeks there, which then extended to three. It was a unique situation, as I stayed with the couple that had invited me to teach at their dance studio. It was a Black American woman and her Danish husband. Their house was huge, and their yard was full of cherry trees. On my day off, we made cherry pies, and they introduced me to other friends. It was a good three weeks.

When I first arrived, my hosts picked me up and showed me my room, telling me to get settled and then come down when I was ready. What they didn't tell me was that they were Buddhist and that they would be chanting. I had no issue with them being

Buddhist; I just didn't know when to come down, so I stayed quiet for the next hour so as not to interrupt. It was not the first time I heard the Buddhist chants; many of my friends were also Buddhist, and I would always admire the beauty of their altars and the chants.

After an hour, they came up and knocked on the door, asking why I hadn't come down. I said it was out of respect. They apologized for not sharing with me that they were Buddhist and invited me to move around freely. I was not offended; I took it as an excellent opportunity to learn. Staying with them also allowed me to see more of Denmark and meet other people. It was a wonderful experience, personally and professionally.

After I visited Denmark, I was invited to teach in Finland, which was also an amazing experience. I received an invitation to stay for a full-year contract as a guest dance teacher, but I did not want to live six months in darkness and six months in the sun. So, I said "no" and left when the contract was finished.

My dream was to live in Paris. While living in Vienna, I worked with a photographer who went back and forth between Vienna and Paris. He kept telling me that where he stayed was not a fit for me, but I was determined to get to Paris. I went to visit and stayed with an American dancer who had been living there for a few years. When I arrived, something in my spirit told me I was home. Paris had been calling me since I was a kid, maybe because the French dancers could do no wrong in the US, even if they were not as strong of dancers. I didn't know why, I just knew I needed to be in Paris.

After the visit, I bugged the photographer until he finally gave in and introduced me to the person who owned the house where he stayed in France. Notice I said France and not Paris. The house was a bit outside of Paris, maybe thirty-five to forty minutes on the train. I said bye to Vienna and booked a flight on Iranian Airlines. It was the cheapest airline, and I thought, *Hey, it's only an hour. Why spend all that money?*

I had big suitcases. I boarded this plane, and the seats were taped up with duct tape. After we were seated, armed men got on board and went up and down the aisles. I was sitting next to a young guy from Germany, and we held hands the entire flight because it was bumpy and scary. I was, of course, the only Black female on the plane. I don't know if the crew thought we were together or not, but I am forever grateful to my seatmate. He stayed with me as I gathered my bags, then walked me to the taxi stand.

I had the address of the house on a piece of paper written out in French by my friend in Vienna. When I arrived, it was the middle of the night and pitch black. I had no idea where I was going or what I was walking into. There were no lights on outside or inside the house when we pulled up. To this day, I believe the cab driver was a girl dad, because he kept checking the address and trying to speak English, asking if I was sure. I didn't have a clue! I had a phone number but no way to call.

The taxi driver did not want to leave me outside. The house was big and dark and looked like the Addams family home from the TV show. After the driver honked his horn for some time, a light popped on. I got out of the taxi, unloaded my suitcases, and bravely walked to the front door. The owner had been sleeping and forgot I was arriving that night. She told me to come to the side door, as it would be easier to get to the room I was renting from that side of the house. *Lord, please protect me.*

She finally came downstairs, opened the door, and said, "Bring one up at a time." I figured no one was going to come by and steal a bag as I tried to drag my suitcases into the house. Boy was I not ready for what I walked into.

I kept telling myself, "You want to be in Paris; this is a way to make it happen."

The owner lived upstairs in a separate apartment. She had grown up with the photographer from Vienna and was very nice. She knew from what my friend told her that this was different for me. Thank goodness she spoke English. She showed me to the room I was renting, where she had kindly left sheets and towels for me. It was not a big room; it had a queen-sized bed, a desk, and a dresser. If you know apartments or houses in Europe, you know that not all rooms have closets. I was used to living out of a suitcase. *I'll do what I need to do*, I thought.

My next-door neighbors, the couple renting the room next to mine, were not home, but I could hear a bird as we took a tour of the house. The owner told me they did have a bird and to just bang on the wall if it was too loud. We then went upstairs to her apartment. "If you would like to come up to shower here, I'm okay with that," she offered. She had a boyfriend who was partially living with her, so I thanked her, but I knew I would not be taking her up on that.

We then went back down to the kitchen, where I could have space in the fridge for my items. She told me a French artist lived in the bottom apartment. "He comes and goes," she said. Keep in mind, it was late at night, and I was tired and wanted a shower. I survived the airline with armed guards and seats held together by duct tape. I was done.

Then we went back to my floor, and she showed me the bathroom. The shower was a garden hose, and the toilet was in the hallway—a standing toilet. I also had a standing toilet in my Vienna apartment; it typically means it's a private, small room where you step up and place your feet as indicated and squat over a hole. I settled in and prayed. I decided I would take a shower in her apartment that night, because her boyfriend was not there. The rest of the time, I had to make do with the garden hose. The hotel in Greece was not looking so bad, now. The difference was I was going to do what I needed to do to be in Paris—or as close to it as possible!

I made it through the night and woke up to really see the house. I immediately knew I needed cleaning products, as well as my own kitchen items, by which I mean one plate, one fork, one knife, one spoon, a pan, and a pot. In the light, I could see that the kitchen sink was full of dishes, and the grease on the walls was thick! I could not tell my parents about the condition of the house; if I wanted to stay in Paris, I needed to do what I needed to do.

I learned how to use the metro, get into the city, go to auditions, and take classes to meet other dancers. I also signed with a modeling agency for commercials. The dancer I stayed with when I came to visit told me about an audition for one of the oldest theaters in Paris, where they were casting for a new show. I went to the audition, and I got the gig! The choreographer was an American woman who had been working with the theater for years. She asked to see my visa.

I looked at her and said, "What visa? I've been traveling and dancing without a visa in all the countries where I've lived."

She informed me I would need to have one to perform in the show.

"Tell me what I need to do," I answered.

The theater helped with the process on the French side, and I went back to the States to complete the visa process. It was the first time I had been back in almost two years.

With a work visa in hand and rehearsals due to begin soon, I returned to Paris. I had been hired as a dancer, as well as the understudy for the lead singer. Let me be clear with you: I still could not sing. I could not sing in English, German, or French. When the producers from the Broadway show *Cats* had heard I was in Vienna, they had asked me to audition. As I had before, I danced without a problem, but I told them I still couldn't sing. While I was in Paris, they saw me dance again, but finally admitted it would not be fair to the musical director to try to get me up to speed.

So, when the new show told me I would be the understudy for the star of the show, who was a singer, I made it very clear that it would not fare well—especially not if I had to sing in French. Come to find out, I would be singing to a playback track. The star of the show was a Black American woman, which is why I was selected as her understudy. I was the only Black girl in the show, and there was one Black male dancer, a friend of mine.

When I returned with my visa, it was the perfect time to move out of my first "house." Two weeks before moving, I heard through other dancers that a woman owned a few apartments that she would rent to artists or dancers, and we didn't need all the paperwork. I went to see it, and it was a one-bedroom. *Perfect. Impasse Briare* (aka Shit Ally—the dogs loved that impasse), *here I come.* It came furnished; I just needed to move my stuff.

The apartments were set around a circular courtyard, where I would often run into a Frenchman who would say hello in

English. I would say hi, but keep moving. Across the courtyard was a family, including a lovely man who performed in theaters with his dog act; he also spoke English. The landlord introduced us when I moved in. "If you have an emergency, he will always help," she said. It was nice to know someone who spoke English was close by, because I did not speak a word—more accurate, more than five words—of French.

Whenever I ran into the other Frenchman, he would try to have a conversation. I wasn't interested, as I was always running to rehearsals. One day, he stopped me and said, "You are in the show with a very good friend of mine."

He stated her name, and I looked at him and said, "I don't know her. She must be a showgirl; I'm a dancer." We had not yet come together for rehearsal.

The following week, the entire cast was brought in to start staging the show. This very pretty girl came over to me and said, "My friend has been trying to speak to you. He's a good guy."

"That's nice," I said. I still wasn't interested.

Maybe a week later, we had a day off. I was looking nuts, throwing out the trash, when who did I run into, also throwing out his trash? I had nowhere to go and no excuse to run. He asked where I was from and how the show was going. He let me know he would love to cook for his friend and me. She had invited him to the show, and he would be coming during opening week. He cooked for us, and he came to the show. We ended up walking back to the apartment, which was not a close walk, then we stayed up talking and drinking wine. Did I mention he lived in the apartment under mine?

Years later, I would find out that he told the guy who had the dog act that I would be his girlfriend—maybe wife.

Rehearsals were broken up into dancers, showgirls, and the singer. I had several featured dance roles, which pissed off the French dancers. *Oh well*, that was nothing new. What *was* new was that this was the first show where the costumes were being custom-made for the characters we were dancing and fit to our bodies. It was exciting to go to the Maison, where the costumes were sketched with your face and each of your roles. Each measurement was taken, from your feet to your head, with shoes and headpieces designed and ordered, as well as each feather and rhinestone placed on the costume according to your body. It was rare to open a new show with new costumes.

We were in full swing with rehearsals, and the choreographer had created a nice dance piece, but the theater folks in charge didn't care for it and made her change it. I remember saying to her, "Aren't you going to fight for that piece?" I lost respect for her that day, seeing how she always went along with the flow. I understood she had to do what was needed, but not fighting for something she created made no sense to me. I went from being a favorite to waiting for the show to open and for her to leave.

We were deep into rehearsals and finally got a half-day off. I invited one of the dancers back to my place to hang out and have a glass of wine. It was a small one-bedroom, and we were sitting in the kitchen area when we both saw shadows that appeared to be directly outside my window. We had only had a glass of wine, so we were not drunk. We jumped up and went to the window, then realized it was a group of workmen across the courtyard.

We laughed, but then she said, "Oh, it's just a bunch of niggas."

She was from Germany, and again, I understand "negro" from "nigga." Let's just say I ended our wine date soon after, since she felt it was okay to call them that—then turn to me to say, "But not you, Leslie." That was the end of hanging out with her.

The show opened, and it was a big deal in Paris. Things were running smoothly, and we eventually got into a groove. While I was dancing in the show, I had the opportunity to dance in other events during the day or shoot commercials. Being the only Black dancer in the cast opened doors. When people came to see the performance, they would often invite me to appear in commercials, walk in fashion shows, or dance in other productions, as long as it worked with my schedule.

After being in the show for a little over two years, I was bored. I decided it was time to leave the show, but not Paris. The French guy who lived in the apartment under mine was now my boyfriend. I was getting offers for other jobs that I couldn't do while still in the show. I gave my notice, but the producers threw a monkey wrench into my timing. The star of the show needed to take her vacation; if I left, there would be no understudy. I agreed to stay, and a week later, I began officially rehearsing the star's role as I continued dancing my other roles and trying to move to the next gig. The next gig would be freelance.

The rehearsals went well, and I already knew the part. The kicker was that I would not be singing but mouthing to the playback in French and English. As long as I kept my mouth moving along with everything else, all would be fine. I didn't expect to get sick. I rarely got sick with a common cold, and I usually only went to the doctor for regular check-ups. I had the most amazing doctor in Paris; she cared for everything from head to toe, except teeth. When the pain became unbearable in my stomach, my boyfriend pushed for me to go to the doctor immediately.

She said I needed to go to the hospital; I had appendicitis. Going to the hospital was not an option, however, because I needed to take over for the star of the show in two days. She was heading back to America for a quick trip; when she returned, I was out. I had a plan! Well, God had other plans.

I went into the stage manager's office and said, "I have appendicitis, and I will need to change some of the choreography. Some of the lifts by the waist cannot happen." She agreed, and we called a special rehearsal to work it out. Another part of my agreement to stay and perform for an additional week while sick was that the theater promised to have an ambulance on call. Of course, everyone thought I was nuts for doing this and that I should walk away and let the theater figure it out. But I had given my word, and I prayed that God's plan would become my plan.

Opening night arrived for my "singing debut" and passed without issue or additional pain. I received a standing ovation at the end of the show. I did not know that the choreographer of the show had flown in from the States to check on things and to see me perform the starring role. Keep in mind: When she left after the opening, I was not her favorite, and she was not mine. After the show, she came into the private dressing room backstage to demand to know why I changed her choreography, insisting that I had no authority to do so.

I was just happy to have made it through the show. Tons of my friends and other folks had come out to support me in the role, knowing I was sick and leaving. Now, this chick had flown in and thought she was going to pick up where she left off. I wasn't going to fall into the trap of arguing with her. My job was to dance. I've always said: Don't mess with my roles, and I'll give you everything I have when my foot hits that stage.

I turned to her and asked, "Why are you speaking to me like that? I was given permission to make changes. By all rights, I should be recovering from surgery." I continued, "Nothing I changed throws anything else off, and it makes sense."

By that time, others were gathering around the door to give me flowers. Of course, someone said, "The changes suit you."

Another said, "Look at you, starring in a show in Paris."

The choreographer walked away in a bit of a huff. I honestly didn't care; I had five more nights to get through. I did not need an ambulance for the rest of the week, but I was pushing it. I needed to go into surgery.

I scheduled the surgery for the day after my last night in the show. The last night came, and the sound guys played a trick on me. I would always sing into the mic, and they would keep the sound off, so I could match my lips to the track as perfectly as possible. During the last show, they somehow rigged the mic to pick up my voice and made a tape for me as a going-away gift. When they asked me to come to the sound booth after the show, I thought it was odd because they usually came to my dressing room each night to collect the mics and sound packs. When I went up to say goodbye to everyone and thank them, they played the tape back for me, and it sounded like I was killing cows all the way back in the States. It was so bad and so funny, I thought I was going to be rushed to the hospital at that moment, the way I doubled over with laughter. I had to call a few of my friends to come upstairs to listen. They could not have given me a better present.

The following day, we were off to the hospital. I met the doctor in advance of my surgery, and I was pleased that he spoke English.

My "boyfriend" (things were a bit rocky during that time) was with me. Because of the way the healthcare system (which I paid into) works in France, I was able to request a private room with meals for him, along with American newspapers for me. A three-night stay was one hundred dollars, including the operation and aftercare. And it was only one hundred dollars because I requested a private room and American newspapers. Say what you want, but you cannot beat the European healthcare system.

I woke up from surgery to find my boyfriend there enjoying a lobster dinner and wine (included in the hundred dollars). I was half-awake as he started discussing how we should move in together. *Who did they give the drugs to?* I was thinking. *We were discussing breaking up a few days ago.*

The next item he sprang on me was that he thought we should get out of the city so I could relax after surgery, and that he had arranged for us to go to his parents' home in the countryside. That sounds relaxing, doesn't it? Except I had not met his parents, and they still loved his ex . . . whom they hoped he would come to his senses and marry.

Imagine going to meet someone's parents who already don't care for you. I was American, Black, and about to show up not speaking French, or very little. And I was sick. *Jesus, take the wheel!* It was an interesting trip, to say the least. His mother was lovely, and she made an effort. She was a fantastic cook; she made things that I could eat post-surgery. His father clearly wanted no part of me and kept calling me by the ex's name.

On the way home, I told my boyfriend, "They are your parents, and I would never disrespect them, but I must be very clear: My life does not depend on them. How I move will depend on how I move. I do not want you to disrespect them, but I will not be disrespected by them." They lived far enough away that I didn't need to be concerned about visits.

My boyfriend was the wild child. He traveled all over the place. He was rugged and worked in a theater where he handled props and lights. He was the guy who slept with all the dancers and drank like France was going to run out of wine. No one thought we were a match. People would say, "Leslie is way too strict about how she runs her life to deal with shenanigans from a guy like that." Trust me, we had our moments. Like when I walked out of a friend's dinner because my boyfriend decided the table had called him to jump on top of it and dance. I didn't say anything; I just picked my coat up and left. We were both used to getting what we wanted and living how we pleased, yet we had fun together. I guess that's why his dad thought I would be gone soon, and if he could help me move along, he would.

I continued to heal after the surgery, and in the process, we spoke seriously about moving in together. We started going to apartment showings together, and somehow, between the time he would call in French and the time we would show up together, the apartment would be "taken." It was not rocket science to realize they did not want to rent to an interracial couple. He decided to go look at a few places alone. One day, we met for lunch; he would go see a new place after, and I would run around shopping. As we finished lunch, he decided, "Let's just go over together. This is ridiculous."

The broker was friendly, which was new for us. She showed us the place, and I loved it. There was a winding staircase inside along with a loft space, bedroom, bath, and half bath. I thought, *I want this place!*

I looked at him and said, "This is it."

The broker began to ask questions: "Where are you from? Why are you in France?"

"I'm a dancer," I shared, and I told her my name.

"My sister's name is Leslie," she said. She shared her story of being Jewish and having a hard time finding apartments; she understood that landlords didn't want foreigners, Jews, Africans—the list went on. She was determined to get us the apartment. She told my boyfriend everything he needed to bring to the office tomorrow. She couldn't hold it, as she would be pushed to keep showing it until we signed.

She looked at me and said, "I'm sorry, but if you want this place, let him come to the office alone tomorrow. I will push, and it will be yours. You can add your name later; let me help you secure the place. My boss, if he sees you . . . I will lose my job, and he will not release the apartment even to him."

I had no problem not showing up. I looked at both of them and said, "Do what you have to do." We got the place.

After leaving the show, I connected with two different choreographers who kept me beyond busy. Then, the Black dancer who had been in the show with me called one day and said he had a gig to be a backup dancer for an American singer performing in Paris, and maybe a quick European tour. Would I be interested? I jumped at the chance. American performers were starting to come to France on a regular basis to promote their music.

I will never forget that evening. We were in the studio rehearsing the number when in walked the people from Sony Music with this girl who looked about twelve years old and her mother. I looked at my dance partner like, "Seriously, this is the artist? I'm dancing behind a kid." Turned out she was fifteen, but still! He began to teach her the steps with the cassette playing, which made sense. Why would you use your voice while learning the steps? I still thought, *Geez, a kid.* Then she decided to sing, and when she opened her mouth, I was shocked by the strength of her voice. *Wow, can she sing! I need to pull up. This could be a fun gig.*

It was a fun gig, and I became friendly with Dana and her mom. It was the two of them against the world. Dana had been a Broadway kid and was discovered by a French artist who thought she could make it big in France. They were right; she signed with Sony Music in France. Because they were Black and new to this side of the industry, Dana hit a few bumps in the road with how she was managed and how they spoke to her mother, who was her manager. They became like family.

Eventually, Sony asked me to be a liaison when my friend who connected me with them went off to a different gig. I took over the choreography and brought in two other artists who were mixed-race and beautiful dancers. Dana was preparing for a summer European tour; we would dance at festivals, for TV shows, and make certain other appearances. I would now oversee the dancers, costumes, and choreography, as well as liaise for business discussions between Dana and her mom and the Sony representatives. We had an amazing three to four years of traveling all over Europe, and we truly felt like a family. On one of our tours, we were performing for a TV show in Spain. When we arrived, they had us sitting in the lobby, which was strange because we were typically escorted to the green room. After a while, we asked if we could please go to our green room or a dressing room to change and get ready.

Are you ready for this? We were escorted to a broom closet to change. We all looked at each other and, in unison, said "NO!" We had to carry on like a bunch of divas and push our rep to let them know we would not be changing in the broom closet, and if we didn't have a proper place to change, then we would decline the show. It was crazy that they thought it was okay to put us in there. And yes, there were actual brooms, mops, and buckets where they sent us. When they called us and we didn't go to the stage, they somehow found a dressing room for us. We became family by bonding over stories like that. Each of us understood what it was like to be a Black female performer.

In between performing with Dana and being called to help Sony whenever an American artist came to town, I began to work with a choreographer who had a show going to Evian, France, various TV shows, and small theaters throughout Europe. She and I did a lot of special events, from the Eiffel Tower to the opening of the Barcelona Olympics.

Not only did I dance for this choreographer, but I also became the dance captain and her dance assistant. She did not care if I was Black or American. She cared that I could dance. I was permanently hired as the lead of her shows. That didn't mean others did not have featured roles, but it did mean there were times when the show was built around my strengths. That did not make the French dancers happy. I would always arrive at the studio twenty-five to thirty minutes early. I wanted to warm up, change, and be settled before rehearsals began. French dancers would show up when rehearsals were supposed to begin, wanting to smoke and have a café.

I would get heated because they would have the nerve to ask, "What did you do last night?" *What do you mean what did I do last night?* I thought. We were here till after 8:00 p.m. because you can't count to eight. It's 9:00 a.m. Let's go! That was my biggest adjustment living in Europe, especially in France. People were not going to move fast, and a smoke and café would be included in the outing, even if you had just left your house.

One day, the choreographer had to take care of something and needed to leave for two hours. She was clear: "Leslie will run rehearsals, and it had better be clean when I return." She was not joking. "This piece better not still be all over the place," she said. Two girls just could not get a part of the choreography, which was the reason we were staying late.

We rehearsed over and over until I finally said, "Break, except for the two of you," pointing at the two who kept messing up. I told them, "You two will work with me." I thought I could break it down a different way. I barely spoke French, but dance is universal; we only count to eight, and I can do that in many languages. We started, and one girl freaked out. We started again, and she stormed off, so I worked with the other girl. I sent her on break, then called everybody back in. "Let's go." We finally made it through the piece, with only the girl who had stormed out still off the beat.

The choreographer came back and demanded to see the entire show, not just the piece we'd spent so much time on. We got to the piece where I was dancing, and my role was front and center, so I couldn't see what was going on behind me. I heard the yell no one wants to hear from the choreographer: "What is wrong with you? Stop!"

We all stopped, and of course, it was the girl who stormed off. She began to tell the choreographer that she couldn't understand a word I said, and it was my fault she couldn't dance it. *Even if you can't understand me, you should be watching the other dancers*, I thought. *And the choreographer is French; you can't understand her either?*

Well, the fact that she lied was too much for me. Out of nowhere, French moved up from the pit of my stomach and out of my mouth, in full sentences for the first time. I don't know what shocked everyone more, the fact that I understood what the girl was saying, or the fact that I came back at her in French.

The choreographer, whom I was very close to, fell out and said, "You are messing up so badly, Leslie is speaking French now." If you were wondering, the girl was replaced with a different dancer. I loved working with that choreographer; she pushed the limits.

One of the coolest gigs I had was the Bal de Rose in Monte Carlo, France, which takes place at the beginning of spring. The event brings together members of high society, celebrities, politicians, and the royal family during the Grand Prix. We would dance to open the evening and the season; it was always a beautiful show. I danced it one year and was invited to dance again at the request of the royal family. I was again the lead.

The night before the show, I slipped in the bathtub and had to be taken to the Grace Kelly Hospital. By the time I left, I was in a brace from my hip to my ankle. Some of the other girls were happy, thinking they were going to dance my roles. *Nope.* I returned, looked at the choreographer, and asked to change a few things. I went down to the dressing room, did what I needed to do, and came back upstairs, with makeup and costume ready. I moved all my changes to the side of the stage with a dresser that was now assigned to me. I took the brace off, and when that curtain opened, I danced! The pain was crazy, and I needed help getting out of the last costume and putting the brace back on, praying I could get home on the plane the next day. The injury didn't sideline me for long, though. I was booked and would not lose a single job.

Life was still rolling along when my boyfriend and I moved in together. It was funny—neither of us had a desire to be married, and we were both happy with the way things were going. With all our cultural differences, we always had mutual respect, even when things were rocky. He was and is my biggest supporter.

One morning, after having been on tour for close to a month, I received a call asking if I could get to Cannes, France, to dance with Madonna. I was tired, and I hung up on the person speaking French because they were not making sense to me. They kept calling back, and my boyfriend finally answered the phone. He shook me hard, saying, "Let's go! You need to get ready. You leave tomorrow to go to Cannes to dance for Madonna, and you need to have a Jean Paul Gaultier outfit to bring, just in case there is no time for rehearsals and fittings." He knew I would not want to miss that opportunity. He negotiated for me and made sure I had everything I needed to leave the next day.

In France, they don't celebrate Valentine's Day. Rather, they have White Day, where ladies buy something for their mates. I never cared about Valentine's Day in the States, but one time when my boyfriend made a comment about "silly American things," I had to remind him that I was American, and silly things were celebrated in both countries. Petty, but I needed to make a point: If he was going to be with an American, he needed to do a few of the silly things. He disagreed. He would not let it go, and I was annoyed.

That Valentine's Day, my next-door neighbor called and asked me to come over. I said sure, since my boyfriend needed to drop something off at the theater and would be back within the hour. Little did I know it was a setup. When I returned home an hour later, he had the apartment set with candles and flowers. He was wearing a suit (he never wore suits) and was cooking my favorite dishes. To say I was shocked was an understatement; it takes a lot to shock me, and that was one of those moments. *I'd better come up with something good for White Day*, I thought.

Not long after that, I received a letter stating I had ninety days to leave the country or renew my visa. My heart sank. My boyfriend and I pulled together the necessary paperwork and went to the French Consulate. My paper was stamped, and I was told to go live. This happened two more times while we were living together, and we spoke about getting married because of it. But we thought, *Why change things if we're good the way we are?* Until the last paper arrived.

I was in rehearsals to dance at the opening of the Barcelona Olympics. We realized that all the signed letters stating that I was an asset to the art community were not going to help me, because the government had changed. They wanted foreigners out.

My first response was, "No way. I have work, I have a life here. I'll marry one of the gay French dancers and stay."

He looked at me and said, "You are mad. You and I will get married and continue our lives."

We decided to get married at the French version of the Justice of the Peace. The building was beautiful. We didn't tell many people as we were going through the process. I knew I didn't want a traditional dress, and I found the most beautiful rose lace gown from an antique shop at the flea market we would visit on Sundays when we had the day off. When we told the vendor why I was buying it, she shared the story of how she wore it for one of her premieres and charged us close to nothing as a wedding gift. I still have the dress; it is priceless.

We needed to tell our parents. My boyfriend called and spoke to my father. My mom had already met him on a trip to Paris, and he would often joke with my sister on the phone. He was nervous, but he called home and spoke to my father.

My parents, as always, said, "It's her decision."

"It's happening on the one day I have off before leaving for Spain, so there is no need for you to come," I explained.

He told his mom, but not his father. His mother sent money so that one of my friends could buy flowers for me to carry. It was a beautiful gesture.

We had a total of two witnesses and three other friends who showed up at the courthouse to surprise us (me). We went back to our apartment, opened champagne, and planned to visit the restaurants we frequented with friends and tell them the news that night. We started at the restaurant where the dancers mainly hung out and where my friends and I used to come after the show we danced in together. They were shocked to hear we had gotten married that day. We were still dressed up and danced to Whitney Houston's "I Will Always Love You." The restaurant, full of our other friends and a few strangers, was our reception. We stayed there until we closed it down, friends calling friends to tell them to come celebrate with us. We finished the night at a late-night African restaurant we would also frequent, and reception number two began.

I had to be up and ready to travel to Barcelona the next morning, and I was exhausted when we gathered at the airport. When I told the choreographer and showed her the ring, she immediately said, "Stop playing. You have to take that off." She knew about the issue with my staying in France, as she had written letters for me, but I kept it a secret even from her that we had decided to get married. As far as she was concerned, nothing had changed. It was time to get ready to dance.

We went on living our lives for a while, and we decided to make a trip to the States. I still had storage in Vegas. My now-husband had never met my father and sister. We planned to visit New York, New Jersey, and Las Vegas.

To be honest, I was not sure how my father was going to act. This was the first person I had ever brought home, and he was my husband. Despite my father yelling whenever he spoke to my husband ("Dad, he speaks English and French, no need to yell!"), they were like two peas in a pod. My mom and sister already liked him. We were also able to see my nephew, whom I hadn't seen since he was a baby.

Little did I know (or want), my parents had planned a full surprise wedding reception for us, huge cake and all. I was not happy! It was lovely, just not my style. We enjoyed ourselves, though, and it allowed me to see people I would not have seen on the trip otherwise. My mom's friends kept saying I married the Marlboro man: tall, tan, and rugged.

After that trip, we went back to Paris and our lives. I continued to dance for TV and commercials. My good friend, NNA, who had danced with me on the cruise ship, had moved to Paris to dance in a show. Other friends, from other countries I had lived in, were also living in Paris. Things were good.

Sometime after that trip, I was cast to dance the Josephine Baker, Banana Dance. As you may know, Josephine Baker was an American dancer who fled to France and went on to have a fantastic career with many ups and downs along the way. She also adopted twelve children from around the world. She was very famous for the Banana Dance number. France was celebrating her life and achievements and planned a TV special to share her life story. Within the show, there would be two numbers performed in her honor, one as a younger dancer and one as she aged.

For the part, I was up against the two girls I danced with for Dana, the American singer. They were both mixed-race, and I think there were a few other Black American dancers also up for the Banana Dance role, as well as others to play the older Josephine. This was an invite-only audition, and I was honored when I received the role. I felt like some of my life mirrored Josephine's, both of us being Black American artists who found bigger success in Europe, especially France. It was an honor to perform the Banana Dance in front of her children and those who knew her, and to have it featured in a TV special filmed in Paris. Again, life was good!

During this time, I worked with another choreographer for a series of TV variety shows. The shows starred well-known French actors along with musical guests, and I was hired as a featured dancer. We began rehearsing several numbers for one of the shows. They were doing a special, which meant we had three additional numbers we needed to learn in a short time. Some of the numbers included the stars, who were not dancers. We had intense, late-night rehearsals.

People were tired and punchy during one of the last rehearsals, and one of the girls started making comments about how sick she was of me always being on camera. First, I was the featured dancer, so I was out front. Second, I was not running the camera, so I had no say in what or who was being filmed. Side note: I did go to the camera guy after one show and complain that if another dancer was jumping in the air and across the room into another dancer's arms, that was what they should be filming, not our feet. That one conversation led me to work with the booth in advance, so they had a better understanding of the choreography.

We were given a break during the rehearsal and broken up into groups to get fitted for costumes, then we rotated to get fitted for wigs. All went well with my costume fitting until I walked into the wig room. I heard a few giggles but didn't think anything of it. The woman in charge of the wigs refused to speak English to me. I was fine with that too. I thought it was clear enough which numbers I would be dancing in. I would be wearing a brown or black wig for all my numbers, just styled differently, and the numbers and roles were written in French. There was no need to speak if she didn't like that I was American, or Black, or just didn't like me. She always had an attitude with me for no reason, and she was friends with a few of the dancers who complained that I was always out front. *Hello again, my contract says "featured dancer,"* I thought. *Get over it.*

I looked over at the table in the wig room, and I saw only blond wigs. The woman gestured for me to sit down.

"Non, merci," I said. I asked in French where the brown or black wigs were that had been ordered for me.

She said, "Non," and reached for the blond wig. I said no again. I understood now the game she and the other dancers were playing. I was not playing the game, so I walked out to lots of laughs.

I went back into the rehearsal room to gather my things, looking for the choreographer to let him know what was going on. I couldn't find him, so I went on set. He wasn't there either, but a few of the girls were. They said something smart, and I responded half in French and half in English.

Voices were raised, and I said, “You want the gig so bad? Dance it. Good luck.” I was about to turn and leave when I saw that people were starting to gather.

The star came out of his trailer and asked, “What’s going on?” Everyone was shocked that he was now part of this. Most of the girls and guys had a crush on him, and it did not look good to argue in front of a major French star with a lot of power.

He looked at me and said (in English, which I had no idea he spoke), “Why are you upset? You are never upset.”

I had no idea he was paying attention to us. I explained that the dancers had played a joke, taking all the brown and black wigs out of the fitting room so I would have to dance in a blonde wig. “If the dance pieces were avant-garde numbers, I wouldn’t have an issue,” I said. “But they just want to play around. I’m sick of their attitude and comments. I don’t need this; I have other gigs.”

During this time, someone had found the choreographer, and he rushed back in. He, too, did not want to make waves with the star of this show, as he knew he could be replaced at any time. The star told the other girls to put the wigs back ASAP and to have the woman in charge of the wigs come to his trailer. He called a few other people into his trailer and asked me to please hold tight.

The choreographer and I walked off the set to speak. “I’m used to people playing games with me,” I told him. “Whether it’s a dancer or a wardrobe person . . . it’s just that I don’t have to take it, and I won’t.” But I also assured him I wouldn’t leave him so close to filming.

We were then asked to join the star in his trailer. He informed me that I would have a hairstylist and makeup artist who could work with Black skin and hair, and with whom he had worked in the past. She was French and had experience working throughout Europe and the States, and she could be on set tomorrow. If I didn't think she was right, I could let him know.

The dancers were shaken when they saw us come out of the star's trailer. When we went back to rehearsals, the choreographer spoke to them. I have no idea what he said, but that was the last joke they played on me. The joke was on them when they realized I now had my own glam person—directed and ordered by the star himself. It turned out that the hairstylist/makeup artist had been one of the five witnesses at my wedding.

Racism in Europe was different, from name-calling and pranks to them telling me there was no such thing as racism. Around the same time as the incident at rehearsal, my husband wanted to invite his friends over for dinner. He loves cooking, and he's good at it. I am good at making things look pretty and setting the tone. One of his friends was always suspect to me. This was the same guy who, when he found out we got married, said, "You don't marry that kind."

If you're asking yourself why I let him come to my home, I was about to kill them with kindness, and it was a business thing. I also made it clear to my husband that if his friend said anything crazy or off the wall, he would hear it from me. "Invite him," I said, "but you may want to warn him to watch his mouth."

The dinner was going well. The other invitees may have warned him as well. But let's be honest, some people can't help but put their foot in their mouth, and so it happened. We were speaking about advertising in France, as four of the guests were advertising executives. I mentioned that France had to do better in its portrayal of Blacks.

They said, "African, Leslie. They are lower class, or at least considered lower class to us."

I asked them to explain. They went on and on about how they came and made a mess and didn't want to work.

"You do know my ancestors are most likely from Africa?" I said, "And I am African American/Black. If you don't stop showing movies where Blacks or Africans or African Americans are slaves, robbers, drug dealers, hookers, or gospel singers, then people will assume that what they see in the movies and on TV is it."

The guy who just couldn't help himself replied, "Leslie, you are not Black." The rest of the guests put their heads down, and I saw my husband, who was about to enter the room and knew this guy was going to get it, do a U-turn.

I took a deep breath and said, "What?"

"You aren't Black or African."

"How do you figure?"

"You are *mixte*." (*Mixte* is slang for mixed-race in France.)

"I am mixed with two Black parents from South Carolina."

"You know, you don't have big lips or a big bum. You are intelligent," he said.

"If I saw you and a tour bus was nearby, I could think you were a dumb tourist asking for McDonald's, not wanting to speak a foreign language, being ignorant," I said.

"That's a white American tourist," he said, "but I'm French."

At that moment, I said goodnight. I walked into the kitchen while the others berated him, and my husband came out and told him to leave. I just remember telling my husband, "When I say someone is suspect, you should leave it at that."

I had more jobs than I could dance in Paris. This was one year into my marriage, and we had already begun the paperwork for my French passport. I was beginning to consult more with Sony Music and their American artists coming to Europe to perform. I enjoyed learning that side of the business.

One day, I received a call from a woman who owned a theater in Japan, with locations in Tokyo and Osaka. She said she had heard about me and would like to meet. At one point, I had had a desire to go to Japan, but I no longer felt excited about the possibility. Plus, I had work. When I heard about the shows in Japan, the girls who were getting hired were all white with long blond hair, or the occasional brunette. Clearly, I didn't fit any of those criteria.

Then a friend of mine called. "This woman is coming to town," she said. "Can I set up a meeting?"

"I spoke with her," I said, "and no, I'm not interested in meeting."

Six months later, my husband was invited to go to Japan to work on a show for a few weeks. When he came back, he told me, "I met the owner, and she really would love to have you perform." He had gone to see the show, and he thought I'd have fun, since the show was small. "She is offering you dance captain, the contract is terrific, and they will focus on a number or two just for you," he continued. "Just meet with her. She's back in a month."

A month passed, and we finally met. I liked her; she was a very smart woman, beautiful and graceful. She had been a top model in Japan and had traveled the world. The show was going well, and yes, it was true that I would be the first Black dancer to be in their shows—most likely in any of the Japanese theaters. We spoke for some time, and we hit it off.

One of my final questions was, "I thought you didn't take dancers who are married?"

"I met your husband," she said. "He understands the business and is very supportive of you. If you want to come, the job is yours. One thing you have to do is share an apartment with three other girls. The apartments are large; everyone has their own room. The girl with the largest room will leave one week after you arrive, then that room is yours."

Life does what it does. During that time, my husband received a fantastic offer to help write a book on the Red Sea. It would take five months of travel; the J. Foxx contract in Japan was for six. We spoke about how serendipitous it was that we both received such amazing offers at the same time, and we decided to take them both.

CHAPTER 7

Transitions

Preparing to leave for Japan while my husband was preparing to go to the Red Sea was not as easy as we expected. For the first time, both of us had ties to a place—our apartment, our lives, and our businesses. We took care of what we needed and decided to let a friend of ours stay in the apartment so it would not be empty for six months. The visas were in place; the apartment was taken care of. We were packed and ready to leave. We had a serious talk about our relationship and being apart for six months. We knew each other well enough to say, "You get a pass to see someone under these conditions." It may sound strange to some of you, but if you are going to be in a relationship, be honest about who you are and what you need.

I flew to Japan in coach. It was a long flight. To top it off, when I arrived at the airport at night, no one was there to pick me up. I was hungry and tired, and I wanted to shower. I didn't have a phone to call the number I had written down, and I had no other way to get in touch with folks. I was not happy!

When the guy showed up over an hour late, acting like nothing was wrong, I was over it. Turns out, he was also the stage manager—mostly because he spoke both English and French. Beyond that, his power stopped somewhere between "pass the message" and "don't shoot the messenger." The dancers were French, English, or American, and he spent most of his time trying to translate into three languages.

"We will go to the theater so you can be measured for costumes," he said.

"No," I said. "Can I go take a shower, and we do this tomorrow?"

He ignored me and took me to the theater.

I went ahead and got undressed and tried on costumes, because the person who altered them was waiting for me. I also watched some of the show and met all the dancers, then was finally taken to the apartment and shown my room. There was a rehearsal the following day, so I needed to jump straight in. The stage manager told me who would come with me to rehearsal and bring me to the theater. The first week, I watched the show at night and rehearsed during the day. I needed to learn the full show because I would be the dance captain once I came in.

Living in the apartment with other dancers brought me back to the boarding house in New York, and trust me, there were plenty of times I wondered, *What am I doing?* I had a large room, but once I walked out of my room, I had to share everything else. Two bathrooms were split between us, and we shared a large living room, kitchen, and eating area. Keeping the kitchen clean was something else. The French girls would buy bread, break it on the table, not use plates, and not clean up crumbs, and the American girls would get pissed.

In walked the one person who had lived in both countries and understood both cultures. It wasn't like it was rocket science, but the fighting never stopped. I had to pull everyone together to speak about cultural customs and come to an agreement that the French girls could eat how they pleased as long as they cleaned the crumbs and the kitchen afterward. Same for the American girls. No one should be leaving dishes in the sink. Problem solved. I could not, however, solve the issue of multiple girls dating the same guy, other than saying he wasn't allowed into the apartment. Every time he showed up after dating one of the girls, there were issues—and I was having way too many boarding house flashbacks! As with any show, we had to deal with weight issues, drug issues, boyfriend and girlfriend issues, and to top it off, cultural issues. Some days were better than others.

One of the French girls was close friends with a Black American man who ran a bar, and he was friends with a Black Caribbean man who had lived in the States. They were shocked to see me, as they could not believe that any show in Japan had a Black dancer. They both had lived there for several years, and I was a first. They immediately took me under their wings. All these years later, we are still friends. They showed me around Tokyo and gave me the inside scoop on other shows, living in Japan, and the ins and outs of shopping and surviving.

The thing about Japan is that if you are a foreigner, you are a *gaijin*. It's easy to meet people because all the gaijins will say hi to each other and help when they can. I had friends who were lawyers and bankers. It was an excellent time for companies to build their Japanese offices, and the guys lived large. I say guys because most of the females I met were teachers, dancers, or married to one of the lawyers or bankers; very few were coming over to work for the banks and law firms.

I had a love-hate relationship with Japan. A love of the culture, and a dislike of the way women and girls were treated. We were invited to perform two numbers from our show on a Japanese variety show, and I began rehearsing and staging the first number for the dancers. One of the "important" men came to me and signaled for me to tell the girls to push their breasts up and hold them. I said no and kept going.

He went over to the man who was responsible for taking us places when we performed outside the theater. He started speaking very fast, pointing toward me and shaking his head. Our guy came over to me. I told him, "If he thinks I'm telling the girls to push up their breasts, he's nuts. It's not going to happen."

Our guy already knew it was not going to happen, but to save face, he had to come speak to me. I ignored the man. I told the girls what was happening and to stay focused; we would dance, smile, and leave. That is what we did.

We had a few other incidents like that. Japan has a unique culture. I love the traditions, food, and how clean the country is. But the fact that no one likes to make a decision drove me crazy. How can a country of politeness take it to the extreme of never wanting to tell people no or "This is the way it needs to be?" The biggest cultural question I would ask over and over was why women who held power and maturity still covered their mouths and giggled in meetings. My boss and her husband were very well known and respected in the business world. That said, she would still demurely cover her mouth and giggle.

One day, when we were alone, I asked her why she did that. Afterall, she had more power and money than any of the men in the room.

She simply replied, "Culture. It doesn't take away from who I am."

I understood it, but I didn't like it.

I was asked to stay an additional six months in Japan. In between the contracts, a few other dancers and I planned to visit Seoul, Korea, for four or five days to renew our visas. Before I made the final decision, I reached out to my husband. He was finishing up writing on the Red Sea and wanted to go to Madagascar to see about opportunities there. He would go back to Paris, check on our apartment, and take care of a few things, then head back out.

I went to Korea and loved it. We stayed in the best hotels, explored the city, and tried new foods—although I will be honest, I passed on the grilled worm on a stick at the night market. During the trip, it was interesting to understand the difference between Korean and Japanese culture. I went alone to the Itaewon district in Seoul with pictures torn from magazines of the items I wanted tailored. I picked out the fabrics; they measured me. It didn't matter if it was a suit, dress, jacket, shoes, or handbag. They would deliver it to the hotel the next day. You could have an entire designer wardrobe in the blink of an eye—or twenty-four hours. I had heard people speak about Itaewon. It lived up to the hype!

Once our visas were secured, we headed back to Japan. Within a few weeks, dancers would be leaving, and new dancers would be coming in to join the show. There was a mix of American and French girls. Two of the girls had danced there before, but it was run differently now that I was in charge, and they had been warned that I did not play around. I held clean-up rehearsals, there were new rules, and the show was harder than it had been in the past. We had the best show in town and the best contract. We had large apartments, massages twice a week, and free food and drink after the show from any of the owner's bars and restaurants. Most importantly, we kept our passports. You would read about many of the theaters and cabarets holding onto the girls' passports until the end of the contract. Some other groups also forced the girls to sit and talk with the guests after the show, better known as hosting tables, getting men to buy drinks.

I met an American dancer who was stuck in one of those contracts, and I introduced her to a lawyer friend of mine. She was terrified of what she was seeing and wanted no part of it, but her employers refused to return her passport, forcing her to stay. The other girls were too scared to speak up. In Japan, allegedly, there are two sides of the mafia: those who harm and those who handle business. She felt the people she came to work for did not handle business; she was afraid of the men who came to their show. With the right people quietly calling behind the scenes, she was able to get her passport and leave. They didn't want a few girls causing trouble. I was happy to help however I could. Unfortunately, several places had a reputation for giving a great front to get girls to come work, but then the contracts were not what they seemed. One more reason girls wanted the J. Foxx contracts. We were not a host or hostess club. We were dancers doing two shows a night. When we finished our shows, we were finished.

I became friendly with my boss and her family. I was older than the other dancers, and it was great to have someone to speak to. She felt the same way; as a Japanese woman with power and fame from her career before she married, it was not always easy for her. We would go to lunch and shop, but we were always mindful of the other dancers, not wanting them to know how much time we spent together. We started to become very close and spoke about everything from personal matters to business.

She knew I was enjoying my life in Japan, it was almost time to renew my contract, and I shared with her my doubts about staying. The girls were too young, and I was exhausted dealing with not only the show drama, but also their life drama. I was too old to be living with dancers or anyone besides my husband—though I was also realizing it may be okay if we continued to live separately. She was one of the first people to know I was thinking about getting a divorce.

My husband called and said he wanted to stay in Madagascar and had found us a home and a studio where I could teach dance. I finished out my contract with a promise to come back, but I needed time to return to Paris, get my shots, change clothes, and then join him in Madagascar.

I headed back to Paris from Japan. The guy who had been staying in our apartment in Paris had disappeared. We heard nothing from him, and now I knew why. When I walked into the apartment, half of our stuff was missing. I was able to get hold of my husband, as I was scared to be in the apartment alone, not knowing if the guy or someone else was coming back. My husband called a friend who showed up to stay with me that evening. I had so much to do in a short time before I needed to leave for Madagascar, and my French was still shaky at best. My brother-in-law came by the next morning. He wanted to kill the guy who had taken our stuff. He changed the locks and helped me to clean the apartment, along with arranging for me to get the shots I needed to travel. He was a godsend.

Meanwhile, my husband kept calling to make sure I was alright and getting ready for the trip. He told me not to bring fancy or designer clothing, to leave my jewelry with his brother, and to tape the money I was traveling with to my body in case someone tried to steal my bag. Madagascar was a poor country. I watched crime shows. *Lord, where am I going?*

I arrived in Madagascar exhausted and scared, but I made it through customs without issue. My husband was there to pick me up. It was weird how we had spent birthdays, Christmas, and our anniversary away from each other, but it was like we didn't miss a beat. We checked into a four-star hotel, the best at that time in Madagascar. He had our itinerary planned out for the next three weeks. We would be traveling to two other cities so I could get a feel for the country he seriously wanted to speak to me about moving to.

After checking in, we settled in and relaxed for the day. The next day, we went into town, and I noticed how the locals were staring at me. Maybe it was the way I dressed. Afterall, we were the same color, but I was clearly not from there. I didn't pay much attention to it. The hotel toilet paper was so hard, I used it to write letters home because no one would believe me otherwise. We went to the big supermarket where the wealthy shopped, and it was sad to see that they had such an enormous supermarket just for them, even though very few families were wealthy enough to shop there. It was geared towards tourists, who at that time were mainly white American men looking to have fun with the local girls, or European men looking for the same thing as they vacationed. It was a poor city, yet it was the capital. I wondered what the other cities looked like. The food was full of flavor, and the market was vibrant.

I tried to keep an open mind, but deep in my spirit, I knew this was not the place for me. I could not see myself living there, yet I wanted to take it all in. My husband was excited about the people he had met and what our lives could be like there. It bothered me how someone could live in the middle of poverty and speak about how they invested in other places, but not invest in their own community. Every day we stayed in the capital, we fed over twenty kids bowls of rice for two dollars. One little boy started calling us mom and dad; he was smart and asked me a lot of questions about America. Scam or no scam, I made sure that kid had extra to eat plus some left over to go share with friends or family. I didn't care, as long as he saw kindness from someone for even a limited time.

We stayed in the capital for about a week, then headed off to the Sava region, where vanilla is grown. It was beautiful, but still not for me. Even though I was the same color as the people in Madagascar, I was not one of them. I was with a white guy, and therefore, I was trash. One day, I left the hotel to cross the street to pick up croissants from the local bakery. I barely made it across the street without being verbally attacked. The people on the street yelled that I thought I was better than them, that I was trash for being with a white man. It went on and on. I just turned around and went back to the hotel; I kept thinking about how everyone had said it was dangerous there.

I was heated when my husband said, "Maybe you didn't understand it all in French. There are so many mixed-race couples here."

I looked at him and said, "Are you serious? There are white men here paying women to be with them. That is not the same as us being married!" Yet to the locals, it was all the same. The sad thing for me was that I understood why the women would hang out with those men. It meant that, for a few weeks, they would get gifts, have their hair done, eat in proper restaurants, and be taken care of. As long as the guy wasn't a jerk or abusive in any way, I got it; it's called survival.

We decided to go to the market with a local couple my husband had met while spending time there. The name-calling wasn't as bad, but it was there. We stopped for drinks, and by this point, I was clear that this was not going to be the place for me. When we got back to the hotel, my husband asked me to grab the key, and he ran up the stairs to use the restroom. I went up to the front desk. We had been staying there for three days, and I had not seen the man at the desk. As my husband was running up the stairs, the man yelled to him in French, "You aren't supposed to take 'this type' of girl upstairs."

Before he could get back down the stairs, I said (in French), "Excuse me?"

He ignored me and tried to speak over me loudly. If you remember, when I'm pushed, French comes up and out from the bottom of my belly. I lost it!

I started yelling in French, "How dare you call me a whore! Are you calling all the Black women you see with white men whores? Your mother, sisters. You are disgusting."

My husband came back down, looked at the man at the desk, and shook his head. "Big mistake," he said.

At this point, the people sitting out on the patio bar and restaurant had stood up to see what was happening. I started asking for the manager (I know, I know), with whom I'd had a long conversation that morning. The hotel showed the French variety shows that I danced for, and I happened to be on several times the night before and the following morning on two of the main channels. People had begun to ask if I was the American dancer who was on the TV shows. I went from being a whore to a star for everyone except the guy who didn't have a clue who I was. I don't know what happened to him, but he was removed from the front desk for the remainder of my stay. I did not want him fired; I wanted him to have the decency not to judge every Black woman he saw with a white man and to respect the ones who were, regardless of their situation.

My husband and I got into a big fight that night about living somewhere I would not be respected, somewhere where I couldn't make a difference about the poverty. I told him it was not the place I felt in my spirit. He could stay, but I would not. "Maybe we should think about divorcing," I said. I had already started my papers in France for dual nationality. I thought I wanted to live in France, but if I had to stay married, it was not going to happen.

I called and told my family I was ending the trip. I was heading back to Paris and then back to Japan. I knew it was the end of the marriage, even if neither of us officially announced it. Going back to Paris was bittersweet. I didn't have my French citizenship, but I thought, *Oh well, I tried.* My brother-in-law and our friend's son helped me clean up a few details. I repacked and went back to Japan for contract number three.

CHAPTER 8

Big Boss

I was back in Japan for Cherry Blossom season, my favorite time of year to be there. We had a few new girls, a few new numbers, and all the same old issues. I started to think about retiring from dancing. I was done living with people, and it was time for me to think about what was next. I started dropping hints to the owner of the theater that this would be my last contract. I still wasn't sure what I would do, but as I passed an abandoned building, I was sure that it would become my theater. I had the music and choreography in my head. I had the color of the inside of the theater. I knew what I wanted.

One day, the owner and I were out for lunch, and I shared my idea with her. She told me the big company known for that type of show had come and taken meetings in Japan, but they could never come to terms with anyone. In Japan, if you are not Japanese and want to own a business, you must have Japanese partners. I asked what went wrong with their pitch. Basically, they had wanted to come to Japan as they did in any other country and do things their way. You are not going to come to Japan and be successful by thinking you are going to do it your way. Japan is a country with a unique culture and customs. That conversation gave me more fuel to design the show.

I had time on my hands, and I loved to explore the shopping areas. Japanese fashion is unique; you can find classic designers or local designers, along with tons of anime and Hello Kitty. I was the only Black girl living in Tokyo outside of the Army Base. Add to that the fact that I was in the show, on TV, and in magazines, and it was hard to miss me. I began to notice that whenever I went shopping, young Japanese girls would follow me. I started using them as my unofficial focus group for the theater that I did not have but would soon (at least in my head). Plus, after living in Japan for a little over two years, I was curious: What did girls and young women do for fun?

I started asking questions. I figured, *Hey, if you are going to follow me, then I need answers.* I asked, "I see some of you come to the show in groups. What else do you do?"

The majority answered something like, "We go to dinner or karaoke."

"Why do you come to our show in groups?"

"It's better, plus you are all pretty and talented."

The audience for our shows was mostly men, and it was catered towards men. However, it was nice to see couples or groups of young women there. They always had fun, giggled behind their hands, and sent us gifts and lovely notes backstage. I felt something was missing, and I knew my theater could change that.

J. Foxx had the theater where I performed in Tokyo and a second theater in Osaka. It was rare that dancers transferred between theaters. Being in Tokyo was a big deal. While the owner and I were out one day, she shared how one of the dancers in

Osaka had danced in Tokyo before and had an issue. They had sent her to Osaka, and now she wanted to come back to Tokyo. My first thought was, *Oh, here we go, I'll need to deal with this.*

It was as if she had read my mind because she had said, "I'd like to plan a dinner. Before the dinner, the two of you will meet, and you can feel her out. The dinner will be with the girls from the show in Tokyo. We can observe how they get along, and from there, we can make a final decision."

I agreed, and we arranged to have the dinner in the coming weeks. In the meantime, I was hot and heavy on my idea. I also made up my mind that I would not be coming back when my contract ended. I'd figure out whether this dancer returned to Tokyo, then I'd stay for a few more months, then I'd be out.

The dinner was set, and the dancer from Osaka flew into Tokyo. The other dancers already knew why she was removed from Tokyo and why she wanted to come back. The dinner would be at the owner's house on our night off. Everyone sat around a long table, and I was next to the owner. You could feel the tension, yet everyone was being nice. After a glass or two of wine, we were all chatting when in walked the owner's husband. He was considered the Big Boss here because, you guessed it, he was a man. I think he had forgotten the dinner was planned for that evening, because the look on his face said, "Oh no, what have I walked into?"

He quickly said hello and kept moving.

But I yelled after him, "Wait, did she tell you what I want?" He understood English, even though he acted like he didn't most of the time.

He had a look of dread on his face because I was always fighting for something for the dancers, and I'm sure he thought, *How am I going to say no with all of them looking at me?*

I waved him over; he was officially trapped. I spoke quickly and directly to the owner. "Please tell your husband what I want, and please do not remix it. Tell him I want a theater."

The table went quiet.

"Tell him, and also tell him I'm leaving after this contract," I said.

Now, the dancers were shocked. She told him about the theater, and he shook his head. "No, you dance," he replied.

"No, I'm going to retire; I get my theater, or I retire."

He started asking questions. "What type of theater?" he asked.

"A Male Revue Show," I said.

"What?"

"A Male Revue Show."

"How?"

"I want to bring dancers from US ballet companies, singers from Broadway, one or two guys similar to the Chippendale Show."

"They came here, but it didn't work."

"They came here and didn't understand the culture. They didn't speak to the women here. I have."

"How much are the tickets?"

"We will price according to the seats, like in the States, but affordable for young office girls to come."

"Where?"

"I have passed by this building that is abandoned. I'd like to look there."

"No, I have buildings."

"Okay."

"What color is the theater?"

"Blue."

"How many dancers?"

"Six to eight dancers and at least one singer."

"You should also audition in Europe."

"Okay, London then."

"How many numbers?"

"I'm not sure yet."

"One must be a '50s number. The Japanese like the American '50s music."

"Sure."

"One last thing," he said.

I waited.

"You must dance in one number. You can't retire; I like to see you perform."

"Yes," I said. I knew I would not be stepping foot on stage during the show, but sure.

"You leave in three weeks. You and my wife make the arrangements."

"What's my budget?"

"Make it successful," he said, and shook my hand.

"Done!"

I had forgotten I was there to bring the other dancer back to Tokyo. I saw a shot, and I took it. (Yes, the dancer came back.) I didn't miss a beat with my answers, and I went from being one of the dancers to being one of the business owners in a matter of minutes. As part of the deal, I needed the business to have a J in it because J was his wife's first initial, and all of the business names started with a J.

I danced for a few more weeks, and then I was off and ready for the next step in my career. I couldn't wait to get what was in my head out to the public. I knew I had a ways to go, but leaving for auditions and beginning to take meetings about who and what I would need gave me the excitement and challenge I was looking for.

Word spread quickly among the dancers in Osaka and Tokyo that I was getting my own show and theater and going into business with the owners of J. Foxx. Everything kicked into high gear. I needed to think about who my team would be. The notice went up in the dance studios and trade papers: We would audition in New York, LA, and London. The notice did not have my name listed as the choreographer. They used the name of the choreographer who staged the girls' show because his name was well known. When I think back, I wish I had fought for my name to be listed as well. He had nothing to do with the show, but they thought it could pull weight for dancers to show up.

I began to go to events and dinners with my now business partner as she introduced me to the business world. One night, we went to a traditional Japanese diplomatic dinner. She warned me that the food would be traditional. *No problem,* I thought. *I will eat what I like and pray that I don't disrespect them by saying no too many times.* Wouldn't you know, the first thing served was a tiny fish that was still moving on the plate. I just looked at my partner as she tried to contain her laughter. She knew that, unlike everyone else in the room, I was not going to pick up the little fish and pop it in my mouth like popcorn. Let's just say it was a lovely evening, and dinner was way too long. I don't eat a lot on a good day, but I was hungry when I left.

Back to business. Remember, I was looking for male dancers only. I asked my sister to come to New York to help me with the auditions. I needed her to sign the dancers in, take their headshots and resumes, and be there to help me stay organized as I taught the audition piece, checked out their bodies, and watched them dance. When I say check out their bodies, that was because, one, they would be wearing a G-string for some numbers. And two, I needed to check out their backs and butts to see if they were broken out with pimples, as that is a sign of steroid use. I did not need that kind of issue in Japan.

Because the audition notice said it was for a male revue in Japan, a mix of dancers showed up. Some looked amazing but did not know their left foot from their right. Others were beautiful dancers but didn't have the look. The look I wanted was clean, beautifully trained dancers, and then one Chippendale guy who could count to eight and move well—someone who had a storybook look, but not over the top. I didn't want the Japanese women to find him or the other dancers to be too much. I was casting for the young women I had spoken to on the streets in Tokyo. I wanted talent; the show would be a dance show first, male revue second. I needed personality, and I wanted diversity.

We auditioned many dancers, and I was okay with some of them, but I had not found "the one." Then in he walked. *Lord, I hope he can dance*, I thought. Mark had beautiful shoulder-length hair, but he was not six feet tall. He had no issue with me reviewing his body. He had no issue with the choreography, and he was ready to go to Japan. He was a beautiful, classically trained dancer. I had found him! My sister said that my eyes lit up when I saw him. I'm sure they did—I was happy. I still needed to travel to LA and London for auditions. I found my singer in Vegas, along with a very strong dancer with an equally strong ego, and my second classically trained dancer in London. The show was coming together; I just needed to decide who the Chippendale-style guy would be. The final decision was mine to make, but it was fantastic having my former boss as my business partner. She was used to selecting the girls, but now she was in a new world.

Back in Japan, I moved out of the apartment with the dancers and into my own place, paid for as part of my contract. I wanted to be in a Japanese neighborhood. I felt that if I was going to live there, I needed to live in a Japanese community and not one geared toward *gaijin*. By then, I knew how to get around, and my new home was a bus ride away from my theater. I had stores near me, and it wasn't like I was cooking. I was always in meetings or going to dinners, and I could eat free at all of my business partners' restaurants.

I lost none of the privileges of being a dancer, only now I was being paid on a different scale. A friend, who was a lawyer living and working in Japan, wrote up the contract for my ownership of my part of the business. I was not performing, yet I had a load of responsibility to make the show a success. I owned everything except the name, the theater location, and the costumes.

I knew the numbers I wanted to choreograph, and I had the music. I needed costumes. There was a dancer who had retired from dancing and still lived in Japan because her husband worked for one of the banks. I knew that she was very good at sewing and designing. I approached her with the show ideas and asked if she was interested and if she could handle designing with me, as some of the pieces would need to break away. She immediately said yes, and that she had people who could help her. I had my costume designer! My partners originally wanted me to use the person who worked for the girls' show, but I wanted my own team. I would use the girls' team only as a backup if or when needed.

The male dancers' contracts were different than the ladies'. They would each have their own apartment; we would also have to think about trying to find mattresses for the taller dancers.

They would eat and drink for free at any of the owners' properties, and they would have up to two free massages each week. They had their salary, and all tips would be split equally at the end of the week. I thought it was fair, since the singer would not be part of the tipping numbers I had planned.

I now needed a set designer. That would be a Japanese team, as well as the building out of the theater under my guidance, with translation support. There were a lot of moving parts. The theater was an empty space under one of the owners' restaurants in the heart of Tokyo. It was a great location. It was not as large as I would have liked, but I used every inch to make it as I saw it in my head.

My friends and other *gaijins* were shocked that I had made the deal. The business guys kept saying that no other American had come to Japan and made a deal like that. A few of the dancers had become jealous. I was clear this would be a male-only revue, even with the Big Boss still thinking I would perform a number.

A few months after making the deal, we had selected the dancers and mailed out the contracts. Things were moving fast. All contracts had been returned, visa paperwork was being processed, the rehearsal studio was booked, and the apartments were ready.

Part of my deal with my business partners was that I had to go into the corporate office once a week. I was now part of the executive team. Other than the Big Boss's wife, who was also a Big Boss, no other woman was part of the executive team, and it was unheard of for a Japanese company. Before the dancers arrived, the men on the executive team were not happy about me being around. They felt I was taking time and money away from the other Big Bosses, and they thought I had been given too much power. They forgot that they worked for the Big Bosses, while I worked with them. It was a hard pill for them to swallow, having seen me on stage a few months before, and now seeing me sitting in the boardroom with them and going out to dinners and other events.

It wasn't my issue. It was theirs. I had a show to create and a theater to open.

I was assigned two different assistants who spoke English, one who would relay messages to me from the office and another who would translate for me during meetings. In the beginning, it confused the workers when I showed up at the office. Mainly female, they ran all the different parts of the business empire. I was a distraction. I didn't know how to use a computer, and I always did something that someone would have to stop and come over to fix. I couldn't bother my partner, as she had a business to run. I had a desk where I kept the contracts and dancers' folders, and it didn't take me long to organize myself.

In Japanese offices, workers take breaks together and share snacks. Those were the times when I would be the American *gaijin*, wondering, *Where are the Doritos or chips or cookies?* Small, dried fish or sea creatures are not a snack to me, and neither is something with beans. When it was my turn to bring in the snacks, I went to the American supermarket and spent close to sixty dollars on American junk food (things were expensive due to everything being imported). My colleagues were not impressed, but they were happy to try them. Japanese culture does not like to say no. That used to drive me nuts. The people I worked with never wanted to be the one to say no or make a final decision.

When my dancers were due to arrive and I had to miss time in the office, I didn't think they would miss me. One of the assistants had been assigned to me full-time to help with anything I needed that required translation for myself or the dancers. The male dancers had arrived, and the female dancers couldn't wait to meet them. I took them to see the show and introduce them to the girls, but I mostly kept them apart due to rehearsals. The schedule was strict; we had a lot to do in a short time.

The show was big news, and it had not been officially announced. However, word got out that the owners had an American woman about to open a show that could go very wrong. I heard some of the chatter from the banker guys. I explained the situation to the performers and explained why the rules were strict. (I'm strict.) Nothing could go wrong; the last time a company came to Japan to open a similar show, they didn't listen, and the deal was never made. The Japanese held on to their culture as they adopted others. The one thing they wouldn't tolerate was foreigners arriving and causing havoc, disrespecting the culture. We had to be on point about everything! There was no room to make mistakes.

In the midst of all of this going on, my papers arrived from France. I officially had dual nationality, French and American. I was so happy! I had to appear at the French Consulate in Japan to sign the final papers and pick up my passport. I'm not going to lie: I was shocked I received dual nationality. When I went to pick up my passport, I was told I was one of the last ten people to receive it before the requirements changed.

I was pleased with my dancers, and I thought two of them could be my dance captains. One was pushing hard for it, but the other one understood me and understood that this was a big deal for Japan. I selected Mark. He was classically trained, picked up my choreography quickly, understood my madness, and had a calming spirit (most of the time) to handle the other dancers. He wasn't competing with anyone for anything. I liked that. Mark had a good eye; he began to work by my side not only as a dancer, but also as I checked on the build of the theater, costumes, marketing, PR, and music. Plus, he showed up for dinners to speak about the show to my business partners' circle. I needed Mark to be more than a dance captain, and he was up for the challenge.

Things were moving fast. I was invited to a board meeting and asked to sit next to the Big Bosses. Where you sit in relation to the Big Bosses shows what type of power you have. Clearly, I had moved someone over. The conversation moved into the Big Bosses' expectations for this new endeavor. The Big Boss shared the opening date and mentioned that I would be joining the meetings moving forward. The hatred that whirled around that room was crazy, and I would soon find out how unhappy they were.

Soon after that meeting, one of the men called me to say the board members were coming to the rehearsal. I told him they were not invited, as I was not prepared to show the pieces at that time. The men would see them when the pieces were tighter. That did not go over well.

I spoke to my partner, and she said, "You know, the men aren't used to not being in charge."

"That's not my problem." I was clear. We had a lot going on, and I would not play with them.

The show would have ten numbers. I had the choreography in my head, which meant I had to get it *out* of my head, along with curating the entire show. At one point, I had to stop the set build to change it because someone thought it was better one way when the number was set for the prop to move another way. To say it was an adventure is an understatement.

We were on a roll and getting closer to the show, and things were coming together. Call number two came from some of the executive men: "We are at the door and demand to see rehearsals."

I ignored them and called my partner to tell them to leave. I knew if it wasn't tight, they would try to throw a bunch of "This is a mistake" comments my way. I also was not going to pressure the guys to be ready for show-and-tell until it was time to be ready to show-and-tell. It was bad enough that I had to leave for costume meetings and run to the theater to check on things in the middle of rehearsals.

The executives did not get into rehearsal that day. They went to the Big Boss to say they had no idea what I was doing. "Has anyone seen anything?" they asked. They made a big mess. I was home and had one good eye open around 11:00 p.m. when I received a call: A car would be picking me up to bring us to the Bosses' house for an emergency meeting. Please bring my costume sketches and other items.

They didn't live around the corner; it would take forty-five minutes to get there and back. I had an early morning rehearsal the next day, because some of the guys would start fittings. I was pissed to have to get up and get dressed. *What kind of emergency meeting happens at midnight?* I was thinking. I got that we usually worked late at night, but this was ridiculous. I arrived at the house, and all of the executive men were there. I looked at my partner; she shook her head. I didn't know what that meant. Her husband began to speak, and she translated. The men were sitting so smugly.

Big Boss told me they were upset because they hadn't been able to see any of the rehearsals.

"Who is upset?" I asked. "You or your wife?"

"No," he said.

"Then we are good," I stated. "It's late. Why am I here?"

"The other executives are upset," he said.

"Are you kidding me? Do they dance? No, so then how can they help me at this point? When the numbers are ready for people to see them, they will be invited; until then, it's a closed set."

One of the men started to speak loudly. I spoke louder and threw the book of costume drawings at him.

"Please translate everything!" I asked, looking at my partner. "I do not tell them how to run the *yakuza*, so they do not tell me how to dance. I could pull out now, and that would be that. I will not play games because they have hurt feelings. What do they want?"

They had never seen me upset, yelling like that. I had been working around the clock, and those men playing games with me was it. I had stood up to leave when my partner handed my book of sketches back to me with an apology.

I looked at her and said, "Never allow that to happen again. You have more power than he does."

I walked out and was driven back home. No one asked me again about much of anything, including how much I was spending. I was told once again to just make it happen.

It was finally time to be in the theater. I watched them lay the floor down like I had never seen it put on a stage before. Mark and I had the best laughs at how the set builders were working, but hey, as long as it was getting done and it was safe, we let them keep going. Mark worked with me editing music, too. The editor didn't speak English, nor did Mark or I speak Japanese, but we understood each other, and we got it done.

A few weeks before the show opening, we were ready to allow people to come see rehearsals. The executive group came, and their mouths were hanging open. They hadn't realized that the guys would go to G-strings at the end of some of the numbers like MC Hammer's "Can't Touch This"—or that the cowboy number, "Achy Breaky Heart," looked innocent from the front and showed more in the back. Not every number had a G-string; there were modern and ballet numbers, and a '50s number where the guys would grab an audience member and bring them on stage to twist and dance. The executive guys were so confused. The female dancers came over and loved the show. They were also shocked, because they had no idea I had the sexy numbers inside of me, just waiting to get out. They thought of me as the ballet girl who could dance jazz. *Surprise, don't judge a book by its cover.*

The executive guys said they would be embarrassed to come to the show. The same guys had no problem being around topless dancers, of course. The preview date for the show was set for December tenth. We had a lot to do, including selecting the staff to work. I did not have a part in that beyond giving directions. I wanted young staff members who would be respectful of the ladies who came to the show. I also wanted both men and women, as I wanted the ladies to be comfortable when they arrived, during the show, and when they were leaving. I wanted *J. Men's* to be a full experience. We trained staff on how to answer the phone and give greetings beyond the cultural greetings. I selected the uniforms to be professional but relaxed.

I was beginning to do a lot of press for the show. I interviewed with local press and the press throughout Japan, and then the large international press came calling: CNN International and Newsweek. I was on TV. People wanted to know how this *gaijin* from America came and created something others could not.

People ask me how I knew what to do about marketing and handling the press, especially in a foreign country. I knew what I wanted, and I knew why I wanted to create the show. I also knew I couldn't let others speak for me. I always gave my partners credit; they would not do interviews unless I was there, and they only did a few in total. They were clear that it was my show, and they handled finances. So, how did I know what to do? I used my instincts. Plus, watching how things were put together for press conferences and marketing for the other shows I had performed in paid off.

Not everyone was happy about the show opening in Japan. Along with all the positive press, I also received death threats. They came from people who felt I was trying to change the culture and did not respect the order of things. I would not be moved. I knew I was doing this for the Japanese women. The show had G-strings and sexy numbers, but I geared it to what I heard from the women I interviewed. The show would grow in style and sexiness depending on the audience's response to the numbers.

Those who were shocked that I had gotten this far into opening a theater could not understand how I was able to convince my now-partner's past bosses to invest. It was almost unheard of. They'd seen the movies; people thought all businesses were unsavory. I was clear walking into the deal: There would be the books that I saw, and the other books I knew were being kept. As long as we kept our deal, I couldn't control anything else. I went into business with the business side of the business world. I'll leave it at that.

December tenth was preview night. The audience's reaction could make or break the official show opening a week later. The dancers were ready, and so were lights and sound. My partners had invited the guests, along with a mandate to the executive men, regardless of how they felt, to also invite guests.

I stood in the balcony area and looked over the railing as women of different ages began to enter. I decided to go backstage one last time to wish the dancers luck and remind one or two of them the right count. "Let's do this!" I cheered. I gave the signal for a five-minute call to everyone and checked in with music and lights. The lights went down, and I took a seat on the steps leading to the balcony where the executive men had decided to stand.

I said a prayer for the show, the dancers, and my grandmother. I also whispered that I was sorry I wasn't there for her funeral. The thing about living abroad and being a performer is that you may miss a lot of milestones. When I received the call that my grandmother had passed, my father said, "Stay there and do what you are meant to be doing. We understand, and so would she." I still say to this day that she was with me in Japan. The Southern woman who didn't really understand what I was doing passed by me that night. A calm came over me as the lights went on, and *J. Men's* Tokyo was born.

The night was a success! Women were surprised and happy, and the press gave us excellent reviews. Women started selecting their favorite dancer, and the word was out. The energy was unlike typical Japanese society. There were emotions and smiles;

the women let their guards down and had fun. The executive men were surprised and happy to feel the joy from the audience of women and see how they reacted to the male dancers. They were shocked, since they hadn't thought it could work. I always knew it would.

There was a new show in town, and it wasn't like the others.

I went from ruining the country to creating a new era of entertainment. The Big Boss realized why I didn't need to dance in the show. It stood on its own. The male dancers became rock stars. Lord, I had no idea I would create this frenzy. Within a few weeks of the opening, women began to figure out which seats the dancers went to for their dance partners for the '50s number, and those seats sold out quickly. Women of all ages and economic statuses were flocking to the show. Grandma in her kimono would be seated in the front row, young ladies who worked in offices would save up to come. Those young ladies didn't make a lot of money, but they were the repeat customers. They came bearing gifts for each show. Sometimes they even bought tickets for both shows and would stay and watch the same show twice in one night. I had created a night out for women of all ages. I was proud of the success of the show, and I was already thinking of the upcoming changes in the next six months.

With the show sold out for months, the same executive men all of a sudden wanted to be my best friend. They could not override me with regard to seating or standing-only slots. When they handed their business cards out at meetings and people saw the J. Men's logo was part of the franchise, they wanted tickets. The business card is powerful in Japan, depending on your title or where you work. It's called *meishi* power! The J. Men's name and logo held power. The men would come to me asking if they could squeeze in their "friend and her friend" for standing room.

When I could, I did.

The show became so popular that we opened a second location in Fukuoka, Japan. That meant I needed to go back on the road and audition dancers again. I needed to fill out both shows. My business partner and I went to Australia, London, Paris, New York, and LA. We held auditions for both the female show and the male show. By this time, there was no need to use the other choreographer's name to grab dancers' attention. Both contracts were strong, and if you wanted to dance in Japan, we were the contract to have.

As the show grew, the numbers became a bit sexier; the audience was demanding it. Whoever said men get along better lied. I often had to break up fights, and the guys were slick, keeping Mark on his toes. I had to leave a lot of responsibility to Mark as I traveled all over and grew the business. One night, I surprised the men and arrived back early from a trip. I didn't tell anyone I was back, even Mark. I waited for the show to start and watched to see how things looked. I still remember the look on their faces when I slid into my seat on the steps and flashed a five-dollar sign, which meant if they made mistakes, they would be fined five dollars for every mistake they made after the third time. I saw one of the guys half-flash his penis as he exited the stage. Before he could hit the bathroom to pee, I was standing next to him. I vowed that I would not only dock him much more than five dollars if I ever saw him playing around on stage for any reason, let alone trying to be slick doing a little flash, but I would also send him home to the US immediately.

All he could say was, "Can you yell at me after I finish peeing?"

"No, I cannot," I said, "and if your back doesn't clear up in two weeks, you are also being sent home." I realized he was back on steroids, and that was a serious no.

When we opened the second theater, I made the hard decision to have Mark stay in Fukuoka. I needed someone strong who knew the show and could handle the guys to oversee costumes and the business for me. I was becoming weary of dealing with dancers. I had done what I set out to do in Japan; I did more than what I expected. I started to think about what was next. I was busy between the two theaters, traveling for auditions, choreographing both shows, and designing costumes with a well-known Japanese clothing designer for one of the numbers, "I'm Too Sexy for My Shirt." I was tired.

After many years abroad, I went back to the US, visiting my parents and making a quick trip to New York. While I was there, I saw Oprah Winfrey and Maya Angelou on TV. I was surprised. I thought, *Maybe America knows how to work with Black women now?* I began to think about coming back to the States. What would I do? I didn't know, but I was sure that I would walk away from dancing and the dance world when I left Japan.

I returned to Japan with an uneasy feeling. I was still in demand to take meetings with Japanese companies. They felt I was somehow able to understand the market, that maybe if they shared their idea with me, I would make them money. I was making $20,000 a meeting to just hear an idea, whether I said yes or no to the project. Nothing was exciting me, but I was getting closer to making my decision about my next steps. I started thinking about producing for television.

When I made the announcement that I would be leaving in a month and Mark would be in charge, people were shocked. One of the English women who wrote for a magazine asked me how I could leave with the power that I had. No other company or *gaijin* had come and done what I did. Why would I leave at the height of it all? My response is that I did what I came to do.

When I said my goodbyes to Japan with no regrets and headed back to the US, I had nothing else to prove.

CHAPTER 9

America, Show Me What You Got!

After thirteen and a half years away, I was back in America. I moved to my parents' house in New Jersey to regroup. My goal was to produce for TV: *60 Minutes*, *Dateline*, *The Oprah Winfrey Show*. I planned to rework my resume, which, of course, consisted of dance jobs and producing credits, but for theater and limited TV in Europe and Japan. I knew it wasn't the same, but it had to count for something. I began to send my resumes to TV shows and news stations, and meanwhile, I studied TV, paying attention to the credits and who was producing which shows. I knew who I wanted to work for.

A month in, I started receiving letters saying that my resume was extremely impressive, but they didn't know where I could fit in at that time. Other letters stated, "Unfortunately, it will be difficult for you to join a station without a communications degree." I began to look at talk shows and sent my resume to them as well.

Then I decided to move back to New York. I moved to the same area in the Village (go where you know) into a cool triplex on West 16th Street. I paid for the largest room. Two other girls also lived there; we were all working. The one who worked for the "hot" magazine at the time learned quickly that partying in the living room next to my room on Friday at 1:00 a.m. was not going to happen. I was older than the girls, but they didn't know it. Older or not, take them to your room or stay out.

During my time in New York, I connected with a modeling agency and booked several jobs, including one major one. Colin, my friend from Japan and one of the Black men who took me under his wing when I first arrived, was back in New York, along with a few of my banker friends. I had a community from Japan in New York.

One of the big jobs I booked was for Hennessy Cognac. The agency sent me to the audition where they were looking for a model who could move gracefully, and I booked it! David LaChapelle, a well-known photographer and video director, was shooting the ad, which would be placed in magazines, buses, and billboards around the country. When I thought of Hennessy, I thought of France. Well, now, when most Americans hear of Hennessy, they think of parties, the club, Black Americans, and videos. I didn't know the ads would be shown primarily in cities and neighborhoods where African Americans lived. It took me years to find that out.

Once I booked the job, I was asked to do a hair test. They wanted to add extensions so I could have my hair up, as the storyline was about a couple dancing in a castle. I'd been back in the States for six months, but I had lived in Europe and Japan. Regardless of where I was, the one thing I knew to ask was, "Does the person know how to do Black hair? And not only do they know how to do Black hair, but do they know how to add extensions?"

Everyone said, "Of course, the hairstylist does the 7th on Sixth Fashion Week and is well known." Excellent, except most of those models were white.

"Does he work with Black hair?" I asked again.

No one in the room or my agency looked like me. They had no idea, as I explained, that it was different working with white hair than with Black hair. But I was the model, right? So, "Shhhhh." I went for the hair test, and the guy started gluing the hair in.

Before he began, I explained, "I have a final casting tomorrow morning, so this needs to come out, and I don't see a sink or dryer. Oil will not just slide out the extensions, and if it does, my hair still needs to be washed, dried, and curled."

"Oh, we're good," never means you are good, and I was *not good*! The extensions did not come out. It was already after 7:00 p.m., and I could not get to a Black beauty shop to fix it.

The room stood still as I looked at everyone and asked, "Now, how do you plan to fix this? You have cost me a job."

The problem arose because the hairstylist didn't glue a full set of extensions, nor did he have enough hair to finish it so I could look decent. The advertising agency called my agent in the morning to tell them they would pay for the job I lost because I could not show up with hair hanging and half-glued to my head. They would also pay to have my hair restored, and they would hire a Black stylist for the shoot. The stylist they hired ended up being my stylist for many years. The male model on the shoot is now a well-known Broadway performer, and I became good friends with several people from the advertising agency. I'm not sure we would have stayed in touch if it hadn't been for the hair issue. You never know how you will make friends.

While looking for my next move to produce for TV (communication degree be damned), I had the opportunity to volunteer to work at the *Pocahontas* movie premiere. I was asked to escort the celebrities to the VIP tent and liaise between them and the production team. It was a good experience, and I had the opportunity to learn how a movie premiere is set up in Central Park.

I then had another volunteer opportunity working with the production team for the Essence Awards. I worked directly with the TV producer as his runner from the trailer set up outside of Madison Square Garden to the inside. After the show, the director asked me where I had worked, because I should have been hired, not a volunteer. It was nice to hear, but I was thinking, *How do I turn this into a job?*

My father worked with someone whose wife was part of the Hennessy family (funny coincidence). She knew the woman running the dance department at WNET (Channel 13), and that woman was looking for interns. I had a phone interview with her and was called in for an interview. The fact that I was a dancer and she was a dancer helped; I was granted the internship. I would need to be in the office three times a week for five hours, and I would receive a stipend that covered the subway. I would also need to go through the Channel 13 internship orientation and computer class. Keep in mind, I had only worked (using that word loosely) in an office in Japan and had never been taught how to use a computer. I just wrote letters or an email or two.

I loved learning all of it. Judy, my new boss, was no joke! She liked things a certain way, down to the angle of the staple on the paper. Most people were scared of her. I loved her. My role was whatever she gave me to do, including getting her lunch. I was also able to see what the music department was working on, as they were next door to us. Everyone working at both the music and dance departments sat outside the bosses' offices in a bull-pen of desks. Interns had their section. I listened in on meetings, seeing how people worked and what they were working on. I spoke to anyone and everyone in the halls. I may not have been producing TV (yet), but I was in the TV station.

One day, Judy sent me to the copy room to make a stack of copies for her. While I was in the room, a woman came up to me and said, "Who are you? We have a hiring freeze, so I'm not expecting to see new faces."

"I'm Judy's intern," I announced proudly.

She looked me up and down and stated, "Interns do not wear Chanel. Who are you?"

"Judy's intern," I repeated.

"No, for real," she said. "Please come to my office so I can learn more about you."

Folks were scared of Judy. I was not, but I didn't play with her either. "I can't," I said. "I need to get these back to Judy."

"I'm Judy's boss," she said. "I'll call her and let her know you are with me."

She had someone else take the papers back to Judy, and I followed her to her office. She asked how the internship was going, how I got to Channel 13, and what I wanted to do. I shared my story: dancer, business owner in Japan, now back in New York and wanting to produce for TV.

She was honest. "We don't see as much producing that will probably make you happy," she said. "We are on a hiring freeze, but I'd like for you to also intern in the music department. You can learn a lot from them as well."

I shared how I already knew the projects they were working on and how the dance and music departments connected when they could. She was impressed, called the head of the music department, who was not most people's favorite person, and told him I would now be interning for both departments on different days. I was now interning five days a week between the two departments. I learned how to edit tapes and look for certain clips. It wasn't exciting (no offense to Julie Andrews, but I don't ever need to see *The Sound of Music* again).

I got along with both Judy and the Head of Music, most likely because I was in my thirties, so I knew how to handle them and kept it moving. My goal was to learn and produce for TV. Four or five months into my internship, the music director's assistant was leaving, and they needed to interview for a new one. Instead of taking a temp, he requested that I fill in, which meant I would need to leave Judy, but I would be paid at least for a month. After a month of interviewing, he asked if I would help sort through the resumes to find an assistant, as I knew him the best and would know what kind of person he wanted. The rest of the staff laughed; they said I probably did know him best, since I was the only one he never screamed at.

I was running an errand in the building when I saw a young guy wearing a blue blazer with "*Montel Williams Show*" embroidered on the pocket. While I was away, my mom had sent me a photo of the star of the show I had performed in in Vegas and an announcement that she had married Montel Williams. I didn't think much of it at the time. The following week, I saw the guy again and asked, "Do you happen to know Montel's wife?"

"Yes," he said, "but I haven't seen her today. She normally comes in on Wednesday. We tape on that day as well."

"Wait, you tape the show here in this building?"

"Yes," he replied.

I told him that I knew Montel's wife and would love to reconnect. He told me he would stop by my floor on Wednesday when he knew she would be in.

I didn't think he would and had plotted to go to the floor where I found out they taped the show, but he did stop by that Wednesday. I wrote a note for him to deliver with the desk phone number to call me, along with my home number. She called within ten minutes.

"Get down here now!" she said.

"I can't, I'm working," I explained.

She laughed. "Since when do you go by the rules?" she asked.

We agreed that I would meet her when I finished. It was a cool reunion. We caught up on where the other dancers were and what they were doing. I shared about my life. I explained that I had come back to produce for TV, and she explained that she had nothing to do with the show.

"I'm not looking for anything from you," I said. "I already sent my resume to the show."

"It's probably with hundreds of others," she explained. She told me to bring it to her and that she would show her husband, but everything went through the executive producer. I was fine with her making no promises.

A week later, I received a call to come meet the executive producer. She was impressed with my resume. She also stated that there were no favorites there. I told her I was not looking to be one. During the interview, I made it clear that I would like to work on the producing side of things. She told me I would need to earn those spots, which I understood. She also said they were in the middle of the season, and the only position open was in the audience department, greeting the guests. "I'll take it!" I said.

I said goodbye to the dance and the music department. I was one step closer to being in the environment I wanted.

It was the early '90s, and I was now employed with the *Montel Williams Show,* working three days a week in the audience department as a greeter. I picked up my blue jacket with the *Montel Williams Show* embroidery on the pocket. I went out and bought the required white turtleneck and black pants. I had my clicker in hand and stood near the door, greeting guests as they came through the metal detectors. It was freezing, and I laughed to myself, thinking, *Less than a year ago, someone had to pay $20,000 to take a meeting with me. Today, I am freezing at the door with a clicker. No one knows my story, or needs to know, or cares. I need to prove myself!*

I did what was asked of me, said hello to everyone in between shows, and paid attention to what was going on. Once the audience was in, I could see how the staff moved around and who was responsible for what. I loved it.

I only had to work in the audience department for two months before the season was over. Then the producers called me into the meeting where people were told whether they would stay or go. I was staying; they offered me a production assistant role as part of a producer's team. I would need to be at a work retreat and prepare for long days working into the evenings. That meant nothing to me; I was used to rehearsals and show days. The only words in my mind: *I'm ready!*

We arrived at the retreat, where we were divided up by

title—executives, audience, senior producers, assistant producers (APs), and production assistants (PAs). We were told what the network, the producers, and Montel expected from us, how to work on a team, the hours we would work, and our responsibilities to the guests.

On day two, PAs received an assignment we had to work on alone. We were given a list of items and maybe fifty dollars and told to go around the hotel to find the items. We couldn't spend more than those fifty dollars, and we had to complete the list in an hour or two. Once the time was up, we had to report back to the room with our items. "Do not be late," they said. "Eyes are watching."

I took my list and the map of the hotel, and I plotted. We could ask people for things, we could find things legally, and, of course, we could buy what was needed. I arrived back to the room a bit before my deadline and turned in my bag of items. We would discuss how everyone did after dinner, as well as hear from the producers about new show ideas and new contacts the associate producers were able to establish. The PAs would have to stand up and present from our scavenger hunt. They selected our names from a hat and called us up one by one. The show's executive producers, the network head, and anyone who had anything to do with the show (except the crew) were in the room.

When it was my turn, I took my bag and organized myself. I presented each item and handed them back the money. The room was quiet.

"Can you explain how you did this?" one of the senior producers said.

"I spoke to people and traded a few items I collected along the way," I explained, "but mainly I told the story of what I was doing and why. People invested in me winning."

Herman, the head of the studio, said, "You have a bright future in TV." He had not said a word all day or night. He had a reputation for saving money, having a lot of money, and picking up every penny he saw on the street or elsewhere. I was the only PA who had come back with everything on the list and hadn't spent the money. I officially had eyes on me, and they were from the top down.

The new season was to start shortly. One of the PA responsibilities was to put the name cards in front of the seats where Montel would go to speak to the guests. You had better not mess up the cards, and if seating or the order of the show changed, you needed to be on top of what your producer was changing. There was no such thing as drop and go, yet there was so much happening on show day. As a PA, you greeted guests once they arrived and took them to the dressing rooms, making sure guests didn't see each other if it was a surprise or if they had other issues, and making sure the experts were settled. You never let your producer leave something in their office, which was on a different floor or studio; you needed to run and get it, but you also couldn't miss anything that may have changed while you were gone.

I was working with a producer who was new to the *Montel Williams Show* but who came from another highly rated show. I was assigned to him because they figured I was smart enough to handle the pressure until they could hire an associate producer. I was still a PA. Meanwhile, associate producers were dropping like flies. The pressure to produce was ridiculous. The pager would go off at all hours; we were speaking to guests at all times of the night. We had to walk people through the airport or pick up faxes at the Piggly Wiggly. Today, we take for granted that everyone has flown before or can simply email a document. We had to communicate differently then. If you couldn't get hold of a guest or if one wouldn't call you back, you called the local pizza place, added a note to the pizza, and had it delivered with your name and number to call you back. And if they didn't have a phone, you arranged for them to call you from a local shop.

Two weeks into being a PA, I was allowed to leave a bit early. Of course, that was the day that Montel came to the office looking for me. I was doing my laundry when he called to ask where I was.

I told the truth. "I'm at home," I said.

"I wanted to tell you in person," he said. "Congratulations, you are now an associate producer. Fastest promotion ever. You will continue to work with your same producer for now, as you have been doing the job anyway."

I was officially producing for TV. It was not the image I'd had in my head, but I was doing what I had come back to America to do.

The job felt like being on call at a hospital as an emergency surgeon. The beeper went off all the time. I enjoyed interviewing the guests and handing over the best speakers or storytellers to the producer. The senior producers had the final say on how to lay out the show, but I always handed them a show laid out. I was usually right; when you worked with a producer and were the first to speak to the potential guest, you got a good feel for what Montel wanted to see and hear from them. I would try to make the producing part of the show make sense. Once I booked a guest, I prayed until they showed up, because anything could happen. People got cold feet, or someone would tell them not to go on the show, or they would be afraid of leaving their town. I also had to learn to distinguish the best guests from the people who just wanted to be on TV.

I was able to work on more of the news stories. My claim to fame was the time I won out over Oprah and landed a story with a professional football player whose cousin was killed by the police. I had the football player come to New York, and we met and went to dinner. I met his aunt and spoke to family members. I also arranged to have Dr. Cyril Wecht, who was a prestigious forensic pathologist, as a guest if we were to produce the show. Dr. Wecht was the pathologist who was allowed to examine the evidence of John F. Kennedy's assassination. I pulled out all the stops that I was allowed to pull, and in the end, the football player and his family agreed to speak to Montel over Oprah. That was a huge win for an associate producer. I also worked on a show that showed the discrimination against Black people trying to get taxis in NYC.

Because I stayed friends with the hairdresser who helped the ad agency get my hair back together, I met other hairstylists, makeup artists, and members of film crews. I called in a favor for one show, where my hairstylist friend and the makeup artist who worked on the Eddie Murphy movies both came. They took a Black man and made him look white and a white man and made him look Black.

The show was a success, but the prep backstage was something else. The producer I was working with then . . . let's just say she and I did not have the best chemistry. She was beyond rude to the makeup artist and hairstylist. She was mad that everyone was making a fuss that I was able to get the makeup artist, as the Eddie Murphy movies were big. They came and worked on the show as a favor to me—no pay, no stipend, not even a credit. I apologized for her attitude more than once. They were uncomfortable, as she spoke to them like they were beneath her, and I was embarrassed that I had invited them to the show.

The producer would often try to speak to me in certain ways, and I would call her on it, but it was something else to see it done to other Black professionals. I was not going to be quiet. The executive producer was always nice to me when it was just me and her reading the newspapers in the morning, but as soon as someone else walked in, she switched. I felt that going to her on the topic of race when we were producing a race show would be intense. I wanted to think about it and figure out the best way to handle it. But before I could do that, Montel congratulated me in the hall. I was not in a good mood, and he sensed it.

"What's wrong?" He asked several times.

"Nothing," I kept saying. I didn't want it to look like I would run and tell Montel things just because I was friends with his wife.

I tried to let it go, but then I told him how rude the producer had been, how embarrassed I was for calling in a favor only for Black professionals to be treated that way, especially with a Black host. Beyond that, there was her behavior and comments about Black people, or people who had lesser means—"the poor" in her words. I had had enough.

"Go home," Montel told me. "I'll handle it."

"I don't need you to handle it," I said.

"Go home," he said again. "It's handled."

I don't know what happened, but the next morning, fire was coming from the executive producer, and she called me and my producer into her office. She closed the door, looked at me, and said, "You got me in trouble."

"You got yourself in trouble," I replied.

"Why did you go tell Montel and not come to me?"

"I didn't go to him. He asked me what was wrong, and I told him. What would you have done, anyway? Nothing. You would have said 'Things happen when you're producing.' Racism doesn't just *happen*. They were guests, and they were professionals."

I was not rude to her after the fact. Of course, nothing happened to her. We had one more show together, then I was switched to the most senior producer, and it was terrific! I learned a lot from him, and that's all I was looking for: to learn and for people to be respected.

One other wacky story happened with the same producer. Believe it or not, we were working on a show about white kids "acting Black." Per my job description, I would find the guest, interview the guest, and line up the show. The show idea had come from several news stories at the time, with the term "wiggers" being used (this was during the '90s). I interviewed and listened to crazy stories about how white parents felt about their kids, Black people, music, and culture.

There was one young white girl, fifteen or sixteen, who wore her hair in cornrows, dressed in sagging pants, used slang from the Black community, and hung out with Black friends. Her mother wanted none of this! "I do not like Black people, and that rap music is sinful," she went on and on. As horrible as I felt listening to her, she was the perfect guest for the first segment, which meant she would open the show. She was clear that she didn't want her daughter dressing like or spending time around those dirty Black people. She just let everything hang out.

I told my producer, "You have to get on the phone with her. She has no issue saying how she feels and what she wants and doesn't want for her daughter." I set up the call and left the office.

After ten minutes, the door opened. "She is horrible," my producer said. "Why did you waste my time?"

"No way," I said. "We can't find a better guest. I'm going to call her back."

I set up call number two, and again, my producer said no.

I was so confused about what was happening that I said, "Please listen in when I speak to her." I called the woman back to ask how the call went with the producer.

"That woman is Black, and I'm not interested in speaking with her," she said. The producer and I looked at each other. I proceeded to ask questions, and she went in: "Why would you have me speak to a Black woman?" She went in about her daughter. Then, it clicked: *Lord, she thought I was white, and my producer was Black. It was the opposite!* We had figured out why she was so open with me. The white producer's name was a fairly common Black and Jewish name. Apparently I sounded white, and she sounded Black.

We decided to go with it and bring her and her daughter in for the show. Remember, she didn't like Black people or her daughter dressing like one (her words), yet she was willing to fly to New York to sit down and speak to Montel. *Make it make sense.* The trick was on her, because I greeted her at the elevator with open arms to hug her, and she jumped so far to the left.

When I said, "It's me, Leslie," the blood drained from her face. "Let me walk you to your dressing room, and I'll have the producer come in to say hello and prep you," I said.

She still didn't know the producer was white. She was a good guest once she found out, but boy oh boy, producing daytime talk shows is interesting.

By season 2 or 3, I began to work on the news stories for the show. Each morning, we were assigned a certain number of papers to read, and then we had to pitch stories that could be a show. It was my favorite part of the day.

One time, I was sent out into the field to get a story from a woman suing her town. It was just me and the camera guy; I was there to produce the segment. It was not the first time I had been sent out, and I enjoyed that as well. The woman in the story was nervous about walking down the street and talking, so I tried walking off to the side and having her sit on the park bench, but she just couldn't tell the story. As the camera person was fixing something, she and I were walking together a bit, and he said, "That's it. Leslie, be the producer and the anchor person. When you are next to her, she tells the story and is comfortable." We filmed it like that and came back with a strong story. It was the only shoot I was in.

The first question from the executive producer: "Why are you in the shot?"

"We have the other footage, but it's unusable because she couldn't tell the story," I explained.

The executive producer was not happy, but the story ran with me in it.

I also worked on several other news stories. I knew it wasn't for me, because when other producers finished their shows, they would run to the fax machine to see if the ratings had come in. But I honestly didn't care about the ratings; I cared about the people.

The final straw came when I was working on a story about women being raped. I had spoken to close to eight women, and four would be featured in the special. When I was told we couldn't feature the women's rape stories because they "didn't make for good TV," I was done. (This did not come from Montel, but one of the producers.) I went and gave my notice. I explained that I was grateful for the opportunity, and I had learned a lot, but after three seasons, it was time for me to move on.

Montel asked why I would leave without a job. He suggested I stay for a few more months, figure out what I wanted to do, and then transition out. That was a nice thought, but the reality was that we worked as teams, and it would not be fair. I would finish the shows I was working on and then leave.

I left the *Montel Williams Show* with new skills—and amazing new friends—but truthfully, I missed being creative. A month after leaving the show, I saw an ad in a newspaper for Macy's annual events, for the department that handled the parade and flower show. I sent in my resume and, within a week, received a call for an interview with the head of the event department and annual events. We clicked immediately.

She looked at me and said, "You are going to be so bored in this job." She shared that there was an opening in Special Events. That department handled the events for the entire store, with each manager assigned up to ten departments. Young Men's, Juniors, Ladies, Electronics, Shoes—I would need to work with the store buyers, vendors, special guests, and whatever it took to build the event. My interviewer mentioned she wanted to shake up the event department to do things more creatively; she thought I would be perfect. She called the special events department and made sure the woman running that department was in her office, then walked me to her office and stated, "This is who you will hire." I just laughed it off. I had a strong interview with her as well, and after a few weeks, I received the call that I had gotten the job.

I was happy to produce events. For each one, we needed to write what was called a blue sheet, a production timeline for anyone who would be working the event and anyone who needed to know what the event was about. It was easy to write, especially since we each had our own departments. For the most part, it was plug and play. If I had five events in one month for different departments, I would have the skeleton of the blue sheet written up and only needed to add the details and notes. Easy.

We also had to design the posters to put up around the store. One person was our liaison with the advertising department, and they would make sure the posters were ready in advance of the event. I had fun coming up with copy and funny headers for the events. I did those in advance as well to ensure I wouldn't get stuck in the advertising queue with the liaison freaking out.

I would leave with the event people still sitting in their cubicles in the evening; not only was this gig easy unless I had an event, but I could also leave by 6:00 p.m. I'd never had a job I could leave by six. I felt like I had a different life: I could watch the evening news, go to happy hour or dinner. I was surprised that the events were basic at best. *Now I know why I was hired,* I thought.

I worked with well-known brands because I had fun departments. I was responsible for Juniors, Ladies, The Cellar, Luggage, and Fragrance, among others. I was responsible for coming up with events or working with the brand to execute and develop the in-store events for twelve departments.

Three particular events I produced made folks think I had lost it. In the first, I had noticed the luggage department never did events. I had previously met with the tourism office of Africa, and I thought, *Let's tie in a trip to Africa sponsored by the luggage department and the Tourism Council of Africa.* The

Council loved it and agreed to give away two round-trip tickets.

I convinced my boss, and she said, "Good luck, the luggage department never does events."

"Not anymore!" I replied.

I sent an email to the luggage buyer with zero response. I did the normal follow-up emails, and then I did the Leslie follow-up. I showed up. I found my way to the basement, where the man's office was located. I scared the daylights out of him because who visits the luggage buyer in the basement? No one!

After he recovered from me being there, I introduced myself and said, "You have tried to ignore me. Here's what we are going to do together."

Still a blank stare.

"What is your event budget?" I asked.

He looked and said, "I don't do that."

"Yes, sir, you do. How much do you have? I already arranged for a giveaway of a trip to Africa."

"Africa?"

"Yes," I said. "We will do the event, of course, in The Cellar in the luggage department. We will give away a luggage set. You tell me by whom, and I will bring in African dancers to perform. He was still so confused. "Sign this," I said.

"What? Why?"

"You must agree to do the event and give the special event department $1,200 plus a luggage set as an in-kind donation. I will take care of the rest and keep you updated."

He was so done that he signed the paper. The event was a blast.

The next event was for Breast Cancer Awareness Month. I went to the lingerie department with a pitch for a partnership with *Heart and Soul Magazine* and a female boxer. The magazine would bring in the female boxer and donate funds. I would build a boxing ring in the middle of the lingerie department. We would speak about beating breast cancer, conduct a Q&A with a doctor, and do a boxing demo. The buyer loved it and signed off.

Friends from the advertising agency where I had shot the Hennessy ad stopped by one of the events and said to me, "Why are you here? Your talents are not being appreciated." Many people thought I was mismatched with the job, and so did I. It was a struggle to be creative, and boy, did I push them. I was known for showing up in the president's office asking why my blue sheet had not been signed off.

I was met with a lot of blank stares and people asking, "You really came up here?" "Here" being the nineteenth floor, the executive floor.

"Yes, I did," I would answer. "I need this signed off if you want time for me to give this to the public relations department to push for press for the store." It wasn't like I was getting credit for any of it—the least they could do was give me a signature.

Then there was event number three. The fashion/music event was a collaboration with a new brand in the store called FUBU, and the artist would be LL Cool J. I had no idea who LL Cool J was. The brand reps kept saying, "This is an urban brand. It's hip-hop." It meant nothing to me because I didn't know a hip from a hop. The fact that I just spent thirteen years out of the country meant I missed the birth of hip-hop. I do recall sitting in an executive meeting where "urban clothing" was being discussed. They kept saying, "Those people steal, not buy."

I was one of two Black people sitting at the table. Remember, I wasn't scared to ask questions, nor would I sit and be quiet because we were expected to toe the line in a corporate company.

"Who are those people?" I asked.

"You know, Leslie," they said.

"No, I do not know who those people are."

"Well, the Hip-Hoppers."

"So, all Hip-Hoppers steal?"

"No, but they attract those other people."

"Well, who are those other people?"

My boss shot me a look. I ignored her; I wasn't the one she should be shooting a look at.

"Leslie, we aren't speaking about you," she said.

"Wow, why am I different? You mean Black people?" I left it at that.

When the event with the "hip-hop artist and the urban clothing designers" came up, I said, "If I do this, I do this the way it makes sense for the music and fashion industry, not for a scared corporate store trying to figure out how to keep money."

I received no response.

I looked at my boss and said, "I'll design the event and come back to you." I went to the Young Men's floor and looked at the collection. I saw the hang tag with four Black men on it. I also did my research on LL Cool J. I arranged a meeting with the designers as well as the woman who worked with them, who was trying to arrange for the clothing to be in Macy's windows.

All I kept hearing was, "That team is messy." I wasn't sure where it was coming from. Was it because they were considered "urban," and not designers, or because the woman who was handling the window portion of the event for them was white and maybe all over the place, or were people trying to push this event off the schedule? I called the owners of the brand and asked if we could meet. I explained I would be responsible for the event and wanted to understand their vision. When I met them, their energy was like mine when I had taken the chance to explain why I wanted my theater in Japan. I loved it!

They were new to Macy's and to the fashion game on that scale. I liked them, and I vowed they would have an excellent event. We would show them what events could look like with those "urban hip-hop" people. I was on a mission.

During the process of designing that event, I worked with the Head of Visuals. I checked in to see if he'd heard about what I wanted to do for the FUBU event with LL Cool J.

"I've only heard bits," he said.

I explained, "I want to take one of the floors that is being demolished and sectioned off and turn it into an underground nightclub. Keep it raw, have people come into the store to make a purchase, then head to the visitor center to pick up a backstage pass that I will create. I will also work with the electricians to keep the work lights and the cement floor."

That area happened to be in the shoe department. I needed to convince that floor to allow me to have people line up to get into the event, which meant their floor would be a mess, even though the event was not for them. (I promised they would get to come into the event to see LL.) I arranged for the Knicks City Dancers to come and perform, and I connected ladders for them to dance on as props and built stages throughout the space. I also hired a female DJ who was known for spinning vinyl records on her finger and cleaning them on her hips before she played them. Both men and women would be entertained while we waited for LL to show up. I wanted a party feel with the lights dimmed as if it were a nightclub.

The Head of Visuals looked at me and asked, "What do you need from me?"

"I need a few props and a chair for LL to sign autographs, and I need lounge furniture," I said. "And since you asked, what are your thoughts on the windows?" I wanted to fill the Macy's windows on Seventh Avenue with mannequins dressed in FUBU representing the fashion and music industry.

"They cost," he said. "This is not a traditional Macy's event, so I don't see a sign-off being easy."

I was on my own. My boss had said she wouldn't stop me, but she wasn't going to help me, either.

"No worries," I replied. "I'll make it happen."

The Head of Visuals signed on. "Whatever you need," he said. "And honestly, the windows could be fun."

I went to the electricians, whom I had a good relationship with, and they signed on. I went to the buyers, and they decided they didn't want to support the event. That pissed me off. I just looked at them and said, "You can come or not, I don't care, but we both know that's not an option." I went to the PR department, and they loved the idea.

I was called into a meeting to pitch the idea again in front of many department heads who really wanted to shut it down. They could not believe I had the electricians on board; they didn't usually speak to others beyond their department. I explained all the departments that had agreed and those that hadn't, and how I'd moved around them. They were clear that it would not be a Macy's-branded event. I reminded them I was hired to do things differently, not just drop a Macy's backdrop and runway for a fashion show. I came from the theater, and I could make this happen. The FUBU owners were on their own mission to be successful; Macy's was the one that needed to step up.

The event went off without an issue before, after, and during. The visuals department came through; the windows were cutting-edge, showing how the brand was connected to music, with a focus on the lifestyle of fashion, music, and entertainment. We received press from the fashion industry, local papers, and the news. Now the buyers want to be my friend, as well as the others who had wanted no part in the event as I was creating it. It was years later that I told the FUBU designers that LL had been sitting in the official Santa chair used in Macy's Santa Land each year.

Macy's was surprised by the success of the event. I received a call from the president saying, "Good job."

Whether you worked in Annual Events or Special Events, you had to work the Thanksgiving Day Parade. I had no desire to work the parade, but that was not an option, nor was skipping the "big dinner" that honored people who had worked the parade for five to ten years.

Everyone who was responsible for having a float, balloon, group, or car on the parade route needed to be at the table and read through the script. It was a long night.

The evening was rolling along. People were having the best time and were so excited; I just wanted to go home. During the table read, I was supposed to call out when each of my special characters was to join the parade, but I was so checked out that I forgot to call out two of them. I promised they would join when it was their time. I also had to show up the night before for the balloon inflation. It was beyond cold that night, and the hand warmers were not cutting it. *If this is part of the gig, it's time for me to think about my next move*, I decided.

As a member of the department, you had to walk the parade, too. I requested a golf cart, which was hard to come by and usually denied unless you had a disability or were an executive or showrunner. I, as you know, had bad knees, and I was having issues in the cold. The best part of the parade was riding in the golf cart through the streets of New York and realizing that Macy's shut down the city, and people were happy for that moment in time. A very tall friend of mine rode standing on the back of the cart and made it on TV.

After the parade was over, a very nice Thanksgiving dinner was catered for everyone who worked the parade. I looked at my boss and said, "I'm sorry, I will not do the parade again. It's time for me to go. I need more."

While I was working with the FUBU owners on the Macy's event, they kept saying, "We need someone like you."

I heard that a lot, so I just laughed.

"No, we're serious," they said.

"Make me an offer," I replied.

The night of the event, the CEO and I were waiting outside for LL to arrive when he asked, "Would you consider coming to work for us?"

"I was serious." I said again, "Make me an offer." We agreed to meet the following week. Things would forever change after that meeting.

You know the saying, when it rains, it pours? I had two other interviews with offers a few days before my meeting with FUBU. The FUBU offer was very good, but not what I wanted. Then they offered to give me my requested salary if I could get Will Smith in the first six months. *Ha, challenge accepted*, I thought. I did not know Will Smith.

What I did know was that I needed to tell Macy's I was leaving. I went in and gave my two-week notice. My boss asked where I was going, and I told her.

"You can't go there! They're a fad," she said. "You are making a mistake with your career."

"Listen, if I'm there for three months or three years, it's an opportunity to help build something, and I'm good at building a business," I said.

A week later, she told me that technically, FUBU could not hire me because they were a vendor, and vendors couldn't take employees from the store. Except, technically . . . they were so new that they had not yet signed that paperwork. I was safe to go. People were shocked I chose them over the other two established offers, one with a magazine and one with a fashion brand. The other brand could not even make me an official offer until I quit. It was a risky move, but I wanted out. I can't tell you how many people told me I was making a dead career move.

In total, I lasted nine months at Macy's. I learned skills I could take with me, and I learned how corporations worked, as well as fashion brands and their relationship with stores, advertising, and events. I was good at advertising taglines and moving with celebrities and their teams, and I could work with any budget and still bring in a unique experience. I also learned how to listen to consumers and how to build consumer surveys. I left with a lot of new connections to add to my TV rolodex.

The other two companies told me they would hold the opening for up to two weeks; if I didn't like it at FUBU, the offer would still stand to join them. Of course, the two companies did not know about each other, and FUBU didn't know that if I wasn't happy, I would be out. I had two other job offers and two weeks to figure it out.

CHAPTER 10

FUBU, The Collection

I would be working on the sixty-third floor of the Empire State Building. I showed up on my first day in my suit and heels and ended up sharing a space with the designers. The staff was small, as was the "office" I would be working out of. "Benjaman's Baby" was playing over and over on the radio, or, I should say, blasting throughout the "office." The room they had me working in had boxes of samples, a single desk, and someone's home phone brought in for me. It looked like a warehouse, only located in the Empire State Building.

This is going to be different, I thought.

When I was hired, I made it clear that I did not have contacts in the hip-hop world.

"Good," Daymond said. "We need *your* contacts. I can introduce you to the hip-hop world."

But it wasn't enough that the four owners would introduce me to the hip-hop world; it was my job to know what was going on. I paid attention to fashion and how people in that world were speaking about the designers. I went to the newsstand and bought every magazine that had someone Black or of color on the cover, along with music magazines, and laid each of them on the floor to look at who was advertising in which magazines, as well as the placement of the ads. I also wanted to know which "mainstream" brands were placing ads in hip-hop or music magazines. I was not sure what I was walking into, but I wanted to be prepared.

I refused to call the collection "urban." I still can't stand that word. In the eyes of some, urban meant "ghetto;" it was code for "Black." I fought hard for it to be called "Young Men's." That's what the department was called when I was at Macy's. When they started bringing in designers of color—and those not of color but of a certain style—they wanted to rename it "Urban," because "Young Men's" wasn't selling. To this day, people say, "Well, FUBU started with Black people." I love to correct them. FUBU was started by and is owned by four young Black men, but white skateboarders were the first to really grab onto the brand and make it their own.

On day three of my new job, I got the call from the owners that they were leaving for a celebrity basketball game. They had scheduled a photoshoot with LL Cool J; they sent me the address and told me to shoot the next ad. I had no other details. One of the designers would give me the items that needed to be shot.

Before hanging up, I asked, "How do you like your ads shot?"

One of the guys answered, "Shoot up."

Really, that's all I got. No photo layouts, no strategy, just "shoot up." *Okay then.* We couldn't shoot until 9:00 p.m., because that's when LL could get to the studio. The photographer and makeup artist were already booked; I just needed to go be the creative director and boss.

I walked into the studio around 8:00 p.m. to make sure things were set up and talk with the photographer to ensure we were on the same page. There was no guarantee LL would show up at nine, and it could have been later, but we wouldn't have a lot of time regardless. When I got to the studio, the photographer was there and setting up, and there were four young ladies with him.

"Who are they?" I asked.

"My inspiration," he said.

"Well, your inspirations need to leave. This is a closed set, and the smoking inspiration also needs to stop."

LL and his team finally showed up around 10:30 p.m. and told me I had twenty minutes to shoot.

Let's just say that they were shocked when they arrived and saw me. "You're the bossy woman from Macy's," they said. "Wow, they hired you."

Some friends of the FUBU owners were not happy that I was hired. I came in and built systems, changing the way they worked. The founders/owners wanted the company to run as a company, and I came in and did just that. I would get calls from celebrities, stylists, and magazines asking to borrow clothes, and I would say, "Of course. I will send you a form; please fill it out and send it back."

Then I'd get the questions: "Fill out a form? What are you talking about? I used to go past the house and get stuff. I don't fill out forms."

"The company is growing," I explained, "and I had to put systems in place. If you rolled with the guys before, you can come grow with them now."

Most people slowly began to follow the rules. Many called the guys, asking what was up. I have to say, the guys hung in there with me as I changed things. Even if they didn't always agree, they would let me build those systems, and when people complained, they would say, "She runs those departments."

Listen, I wasn't trying to be a bitch; I was building those departments the same way I knew Calvin Klein, Donna Karan, and other designers set up their departments regarding clothing loans. You signed the form stating the artist and the purpose of the loan, and then you returned photos for our files.

On my fourth day, I was called an idiot by one of the partners on the manufacturing side. He was in charge of sales and had a way of speaking to people disrespectfully. He was used to getting away it, mainly to men.

When he called me that, I turned back to him and said, "Who do you think you are speaking to?"

"You," he said. "You didn't do that thing with the billboards."

I had no idea what he was speaking about because I had never received that request.

I moved closer to him as I very clearly and loudly stated, "My parents do not speak to me like that, nor will you. If you are used to speaking to people like that, including the owners, because they're the first Black people you've worked with, you have officially found your match. I will not tolerate it. I don't have to, and I won't. I don't need this gig; it's not my first one and won't be my last. You have just started to make money, and I came from money. Think twice before you speak to me."

He was shocked that I spoke back to him. "I'm your boss," he said.

"No," I replied. "The guys are my boss. I came here to work for them. You are their partner, not mine."

One of the young guys in the office called Daymond and said, "The new girl is crazy. She stood up to the partner, and he ended up walking away!"

When Daymond arrived at the office, I was already closing my laptop and packing up my stuff on my little warehouse desk. I looked at him and said, "I don't think this is going to work. He's disrespectful. I don't know who he thought he was speaking to, but I'm not going to work like this. I'm going to leave." (Remember, I had two gigs waiting.)

Daymond asked me to stay, as I was the first executive he hired. Ten years of shenanigans would follow; I would quit several times over those ten years.

As people were starting to love the brand, the internal office was growing like wildfire, and not everyone was ready. We were working with folks who had been in the fashion industry their entire careers. This was brand new for the founders, but they had a vision. We were a mixed-up bunch, but it worked! We had the Jewish side of the office, the Black folks, the Asian folks, Russians, Indians, white folks, and folks from the Caribbean Islands. We were the United Nations, and everyone had a role. We didn't hire for culture fit; we hired because you said you had the talent and skill to make it happen. No other company looked like that—then or now. We were a misfit bunch of creative and business folks just trying to make it happen.

FUBU yielded a lot of power in retail. We were the hot new brand, and we stayed hot because we kept expanding. We had over twenty domestic licenses and twenty international licenses. I was able to create whatever I wanted with our events. I designed it, produced it, and found the sponsors and venue. I had complete control. No one walks in and gets complete control of their departments like that. Credit again to the guys, because they let me do what I knew how to do. I would go to them with ideas; three had to agree.

We were invited to Passport, out in LA—a huge Macy's event held in an airplane hangar. The year we were invited, Elizabeth Taylor and Magic Johnson, among other stars, were hosting. Magic Johnson was going to be our celebrity guest to walk in our segment of the fashion show. I arranged an *LA Times* fashion interview, as well as a community segment interview; we also did radio and TV. I worked every angle.

In a meeting with the guys, I told them, "I want you to walk out for your finale in suits." Two of the guys were in; the other two felt I was trying to change them. "Everyone is expecting you to walk out in sweats or jeans and a sweatshirt," I explained. "Let's flip the script on them and let them see you as designers." I knew what had been said about them and others when I worked at Macy's. I wanted to make people think twice. "Trust me, it will work." It took convincing, but they agreed.

The guys got fitted for suits, and when they walked out for the finale of their fashion segment, they received a standing ovation. They had just moved the needle. This was a small win. I was proud and happy that the audience was shocked to see them in suits, but better yet, that the guys saw they could move the needle with a predominantly corporate audience.

I made sure FUBU the Collection would become a household name. It was a joke in the industry how four designers would get on the red carpet and do more interviews than some of the stars in the films. I knew the publicists, managers, and photographers on the red carpet. It was my job to know who was who in the industry, and I did. It also helped that most of their clients wanted to wear FUBU specifically. When we expanded into suits and tuxedos, we had the number one rental tuxedo.

We used to go to Vegas twice a year for the Magic Tradeshow. That was the show where you either tried to sell, or you were at the level that you were there for your brand's presence. We did a bit of both, and our booth grew as the brand grew. I produced fashion shows that would run three to four times a day. I hired the models, brought them to Vegas, and rehearsed like it was a Broadway show. I brought a few Broadway show dancers to combine dance numbers with fashion. The tradeshow press department started calling me to ask what I had planned so they could add it to their list. We also always had a celebrity or two planned to make an appearance at the booth, not including the ones who would just stop by.

Mark, my dance captain from Japan, came to help me run the shows. He had also worked with me when we needed extra event coordinators at Macy's, and now he did the same for FUBU. One year, we built a stage in front of our booth. I mixed ballet, Jazz, and tap numbers between the fashion segments. We hired models who looked like our consumers, using all sizes, shapes, and shades. My cast of professional dancers and models was the talk of the show.

I was also censored one year because I had the girls come out with only jeans on. They covered their breasts; the audience only saw their backs. The number was sexy and classy. Word spread quickly, and people showed up fifteen to twenty minutes before show time, blocking the path to our booth. Someone called to say we needed to be shut down. It was great press for us. I refused to change the number, citing the Playboy bunnies and other brands with half-dressed girls where you could see everything. With ours, you only saw their backs. I won, and we moved on and had a successful show.

Haters came after us. After one event, I received a death threat. I'm still unsure if it came from an outside source or someone who worked in the office. I called Joe, who was Montel Williams's head of security and with whom I had become close while working the show. He is one of my closest friends. He and other undercover security took me home that night and moved as I moved for a bit to make sure it was nothing serious. Why would I get a death threat, you ask? One, I handled a lot for the brand. Two, I told a model she could not model for us. Three, I said someone could not get into our party or event. Four, I said no to someone's project. Five, I said no to loaning clothing to someone because they stole from us in the past, or they had returned clothing damaged, or we had too much on loan, and I just said no. The list goes on. I knew I had a plan for the FUBU brand and owners, so sometimes I just had to say no.

When I finally did get my own office, it had a great view from the Empire State Building. No blasting music, just myself and my assistant. I went through many assistants at FUBU. It was not a nine-to-five gig. I was in the office by 7:30 or 8:00 a.m. and would work until late—then go to an event. It was not easy; I expected a lot, and if you worked with me, that meant you worked for the guys. There were always many moving parts to get something done. I needed someone who could hold their own, and I rotated through assistants. I had a few colleagues who could tell if the person would make it or not, and they began taking bets.

In one meeting, I suddenly became President of Marketing, Advertising, and PR. I had spoken about changing my title from Senior VP to President. I was originally told that it may cause confusion with the president of the company. It made no sense, but I let it go. One day, Daymond came into my office to catch up and go over things. He picked up my card (people still remember the red FUBU business cards), looked at it, and asked me why I wasn't President. *Really, D?*

"You run this," he said. "No one is over you in these areas. You are President. How's that for a promotion? Order new cards."

I was always taken care of in many other ways, too.

Our offices were the place to be. Celebrities and athletes would call and ask me if they could stop by. We worked hard; We entertained hard. I was not always the favorite in the office because I wouldn't have staff running in to say hello and jump over folks. One day, I brought Janet Jackson to the office. We came through the lobby and up the elevator in the Empire State Building with very little warning to the building security. Like I said, we moved fast. It was easier getting her into the building than out when the word spread that she was in the FUBU office.

We also had a deal with Muhammad Ali. When he came to the showroom, one of the guys was about ready to strangle me because I wouldn't let him into the showroom to say hello. He wanted to meet Muhammad Ali, and I was in his way. But I had been given the list of who was allowed in. I asked nicely if he needed a sample, and I would have had one of the guys bring it out, but he didn't want a sample. That situation turned into more than it needed to be, but I was used to being the one no one liked. I had privileges they did not. It was my job.

Around five years into my time with FUBU, we were celebrating someone's birthday, with a lot of people in the main lobby and showroom, when I received a call from a friend who I knew was working with Michael Jackson.

"Michael would like to speak to you," he said.

I asked everyone to be quiet, which pissed some folks off. Why did they need to be quiet at a party? I started doing the moonwalk and pointing to the phone. He spoke softly, so I was trying to listen while mouthing the words, "It's Michael Jackson."

I was given the secret password to meet Michael at a recording studio in New York the next day, and then I hung up and told everyone I was sorry, but that was really Michael Jackson.

Daymond immediately asked, "What time are we going?"

"Oh," I said, "you're not invited. It's my personal code."

Anytime I was invited to something while I was at FUBU, I would ask if the invite included the founders or, as I called them, my boys (they were and are my little brothers). That time, I hadn't thought about it! I had to call back and ask my friend if Daymond could come, because he was not having it. We went and had a wonderful conversation. We were about to go to South Africa, and Michael shared his thoughts about the country, his trips, and things we should try to see.

The following is a short list of some of the people we met or worked with while I was at FUBU: Rev. Jesse Jackson, President Bill Clinton, Nelson Mandela, Muhammad Ali, Michael Jackson, Lennox Lewis, Will Smith, Patti LaBelle, and Hillary Clinton. I once had breakfast with President Bill Clinton and Rev. Jesse Jackson—and was then backstage with Busta Rhymes that night. I'm not going to begin to name the athletes, boy bands, singing groups, hip-hop artists, writers, actors, actresses, and politicians. I was fortunate to be in the position that I was. It was not all rainbows, however. Working with celebrities is not always rosy. I'm not complaining, but I can tell you award shows are not as fun as they may appear on TV.

By year two, I had made a name for myself in the industry, and many headhunters called me for other jobs. I said no, but I entertained the conversation with a few. I was able to demand a high salary because people saw what I was doing for the brand. I was asked to head up the women's division for a clothing brand and help launch their plus-size offerings. While I was at Macy's, I kept saying they needed plus sizes for Juniors and that young women should not have to go to the women's department to find clothes when they go shopping with their friends. It was a passion of mine to see this happen, and there I was, being given that opportunity along with a nice bump in my salary.

Before I said yes or no, I pulled Daymond aside, told him I was thinking about taking the position, and asked what he saw for my future with the company as it grew. I was already doing everything I could think of.

He looked at me and said, "Oh, you like to leave after two years." Which made me think, *Maybe I do*. If I feel like I accomplished something, then I'm ready for my next challenge.

"They are giving me the women's division to run with plus sizes to be added," I told him.

He laughed! "You want to oversee Ladies?" he said. "Then great, you are now responsible for the Ladies Collection. They need to work with you." He picked up the phone, called over to the licenses, and told them they would need to meet with me and present to me moving forward.

"Happy?" he said. "Now, the next time you want to do or work on something, let me know before trying to leave."

I did not leave, and I was able to work on FUBU's Ladies, Lingerie, Bedding, and Ladies' Shoes divisions, along with special projects like FB Entertainment and FUBU Records. I was a producer on FB entertainment projects and oversaw the PR department for FUBU Records. (By then, I had staff.) I also received invitations to sit on various boards, take speaking engagements, write chapters in books, and win awards for marketing.

I had to think twice about one other offer when Nike came calling; that was different. I loved the company and what they were doing. I knew they had international offices, which would have been a great way to get back to Europe. I took the first call, which rolled into six different calls, leading to a few breakfast meetings with various executives in New York.

Nike was looking for the next set of executives to run the company; the candidates would go through a Nike executive boot camp by working in various departments of the company to understand how things were run. Nike was the only company I would have truly considered working in-house for, other than starting my own business. Where could I go that allowed me to be me and work as I wanted to when I left FUBU? There would be nowhere. Nike, I thought, could be it.

The interview process lasted close to a year. In the middle of the process, an opportunity came up to run the marketing department for them in Miami. I turned it down. I had just produced an event in Miami. It's a funny market, and if you are not in the know with the right crowd, it's hard to break ground. I felt it was a setup for anyone not from that market or with strong ties to the market to succeed. I was right to say no. I heard that the office didn't go as planned. I had no real love lost if I got the gig or didn't; I was making things happen and keeping it moving.

During the year of the interview process, I received the call to come to Portland, as it was time to meet additional people and tour the Nike campus. They pulled out all the stops to ensure I was comfortable during the two-day stay. I had traveled during other gigs while at FUBU, so taking the time off wasn't a big deal. I toured, ate, and met with lots of folks. I was given a tour of Portland. They showed me the art scene, knowing I liked art, and the gyms, even though I would have gym access at work, along with anything else I needed to keep my daily life moving.

In other words, Nike owned Portland, and the campus was more like a compound. As much as I liked the idea of Nike, I wasn't sure if it would work for me. I went back and didn't think about the trip again until I received the call: Could I have breakfast in New York with someone I had met before? I was now somewhat over the process and didn't want to move to Portland. I didn't drive, and their telling me I could take the Nike bus or they could arrange driving lessons wasn't enough for me to jump and say yes.

I want to be clear: Everyone was lovely, but my gut was telling me something was off. After breakfast, about a week later, the headhunter called and told me to expect a call. I received the call from the last person I'd had breakfast with. He was excited; he told me how impressed everyone in the office was with me and my accomplishments and that I would be an asset to the executive team. I would need to start in the US in the Portland office to understand the company's soup to nuts, and then we could discuss other territories.

As he continued to speak, I began thinking, *I seriously have to decide.*

"There is only one thing I need to ask you, Leslie."

"Yes?" I said.

"We will need you to tone it down just a bit. We are concerned, since we are starting you in the advertising department, and because you have done the job before, that you may intimidate others. Remember, you're no longer *doing* the job but *overseeing* the job, and you're creative with a big personality. Could you tone it back?"

I laughed because I finally saw: That was it, what was in my gut. I knew something was off! "Tone it down? Have you met me?"

He laughed and said, "Of course, Leslie."

I laughed back and said, "Well, what you've seen of me was already a toned-down interview-Leslie. No, if that's what it takes, then I'm good. Nike is not for me. No, thank you."

He was shocked. I said it was nice meeting everyone and said goodbye. The headhunter called to try to save the gig, but I told her there was nothing to save. How do you offer a job to someone and tell them to start by toning it down? She was pissed; this was a year-long process. I wished they had spoken up sooner about what type of personality they were looking for, because every time I spoke with someone, they said I had the fire they needed. *Oh well, me and my fire will stay where I am.*

In the early 2000s, I was invited to be part of the Chief Marketing Officers (CMO) Council. I was the first and only Black female on the Council; there was one Black man, and everyone except me worked for Fortune 500 companies. At my first annual meeting with everyone, one of the questions asked of each of us was, "How do you get your CEO to listen to you and take your advice?" People shared how they did presentations, what worked, and what didn't.

When it was my turn, everyone said, "Leslie, your CEO does things my CEO would never do, and he appears on magazine covers and TV. How do you do it?"

I explained: With a straight face, I let him know how sexy he would be. That's it. That's all. There were no presentations, no extra anything.

*

We were making it happen, and our South African license wanted to bring us to South Africa for the opening of the FUBU store there. At that time, other than Donna Karan, we were the only American designers who came to visit for their store opening. It was decided that only two of the FUBU guys would go with me for the store opening and four-day press tour.

I came into the office, pulled the guys into a meeting, and said, "I'm not feeling great about this trip." Something was not sitting right.

We called our license over there, and I said, "I need details for this trip. I don't feel like this is a trip where we jump on a plane and all is well. I've heard the everyday dangerous crime stories. The store has been robbed twice, and it's not even open yet. How do you plan on keeping us safe?"

After a few days, he came back with a plan, which would include each of us having our own security guard. These gentlemen were not ordinary security. They were military ninjas! Before the car stopped, they were out of the car and coming from the back of the place, venue, and restaurant, greeting us at the front. It was something else!

We were treated wonderfully. Meeting Nelson Mandela was on the schedule. That's all I wanted out of the trip. Of course, I needed the work to flow smoothly too. A few companies had helped sponsor the trip, including a local mobile company and Coca-Cola. I reminded the guys to slide that into interviews when possible. The store was located in a beautiful mall. The issue was that most of the people who came to see and meet the guys could not afford anything in the shop and out of respect, would not come into the store. They stood around it, and it felt like we were in a glass cage.

I told our security, "Please go out and move the crowd back a bit so the guys have room to say hello to people. The guys are coming out."

"Leslie, are you sure?" they said.

"Yes, we did not come all this way to look at people through a glass box. We did not come all this way to come and look at people who look like us and not say thank you. Do what you need to do."

They did. I cried. All people wanted to do was thank us for coming, thank us for being an example. *No, thank you.*

We took time to go on safari, tried animal jerky (this was when I ate meat), and went to Soweto, which was the first time our contact had been there. The first dinner where we were supposed to meet Nelson Mandela didn't happen. He had to leave town and sent his grandson to welcome us. He was lovely, and we had four more days to hopefully meet Mandela. His grandson hung out with us in the evenings.

Someone local had been hired to put our fashion show together. I had Keith and J with me, both the fashion guys of the group, with different styles. We came in and flipped the show the way we would have in the States. We changed some of the music, and I had white and Black models walking together, which was still rare. They were in shows together, but not as a couple coming down the runway.

Nelson's grandson thought it would be fun to be in the show. I said, "Let's do it." He was tall and young. I also thought it would be amazing to go back to the States and say we'd had Nelson

Mandela's grandson in the show. It may not mean much in South Africa, because there are a lot of grandkids, but in the States? Press gold! I edited a new piece of music, and we planned for him to walk at the end of the show. However, he went home and told his family, which clearly didn't go over well because I received a call saying he could not walk. It would look like he was supporting one foreign company over another. I was disappointed, changed the show back, and we still had a great show and after-party.

We were supposed to head back to the States when we were invited to Cape Town for three days. It would be a working vacation. We did more press and met other people. Our hosts were whispering that they wanted to take the guys to a club. I wanted to go—of course I wanted to know what a strip club in South Africa could be like, as long as it wasn't one that had women doing tricks. I sat next to the owner of the club, and when one of the girls was performing, I leaned over and said, "She's your money-maker." He was surprised. I told him I owned the first male revue show in Japan. I had been to many strip clubs while researching.

After three days in Cape Town, it was time to pack up, as we were leaving the next night. We were buying our last souvenirs when security received a call that Nelson Mandela was home, and we were invited to stop by. We had a two-hour timeframe; it would take us two hours to get to him if we left at that moment, and we still needed to pull our stuff together. We did so and jumped on the road.

We made it a little later after the two hours. We were invited into his home, and I was able to sit next to Mandela as he told us what he knew about the company and asked questions. Then he said, "You have come home with such pride!" I cried just a little.

We took pictures. The only thing missing was the safety pin that I usually fastened on the top of my Donna Karan wrap dress. (If you've seen the pictures, you will understand—not that I have much to flash. But it was close.)

Meeting Nelson Mandela at his home is one of the highlights of my life. Muhammad Ali comes in close behind him, but I will always cherish meeting Mandela and his grandson and opening the store in South Africa.

While visiting other prominent people during that trip, I had the hardest time with the image of big mansions across from a dirt road and a shanty town, with people living under metal roofs, washing in tin buckets, and barely surviving. I could never open my door and see that every day and not fight to change the system somehow. I can still see the woman staring at us as we arrived at one person's home; honestly, all I wanted to do was go speak with her.

While I was at FUBU, two achievements took a lot of time to actualize. First was the CNN piece where they not only filmed us in New York, but also followed us to LA as we shot the first FUBU commercial, which was filmed underwater. I knew the reporter from my Macy's and Montel days. She was interested in a FUBU story when I first pitched her, but her boss was not. We stayed in touch, and I shared with her about our growth and how we would be filming a fashion show underwater as our first commercial. She pitched it to her boss, and we ended up with a fantastic story.

The second achievement was the Essence Award from *Essence Magazine*. No company had been a recipient, as the reward was set for individuals. I was put in contact with the person who handled selecting the honorees. I pulled so much together for them and had numerous meetings. The guys had no idea. I worked on it for close to a year when, finally, I was told they would be nominated. At first, they didn't get the gravity of the award or that they were the first company to receive it. It took a few weeks for it to sink in. Once the announcement came out and they saw their names listed with icons they grew up with, reality hit: They had reached a new level of success.

All was going well until an incorrect article came out saying the founders had sold drugs when they were young. It was written by a reporter from a prominent paper whom I granted an interview, and they went rogue. I needed to go into spin doctor mode, and that I did. I also needed help from a few colleagues who had been in the industry and were well respected. One in particular really went to bat for me and the guys. In the end, the people behind the awards realized the article was incorrect, and the guys were still honored.

I went all in on that one, only to have someone try to swoop in and take credit. But people knew who had done the work and who made it happen. Sometimes, you have to let people jump up and down and pretend to be shiny. The people who know, know. Despite all the drama, the guys enjoyed the award ceremony with their families, and I invited my parents. That was a proud moment we were able to share.

Six or seven years into my time at FUBU, I went back to Japan to open FUBU stores there with the owners. I told our contact I had lived in Japan and owned J. Men's Tokyo. Our contact must have said something to the Big Boss, because he came into the meeting with the Japanese license, speaking in English and Japanese, saying, "Whatever she wants, she gets. She knows how to make money." He bowed to me, turned, and left the room.

The FUBU guys were shocked, and the Japanese men were even more so. Needless to say, the trip was successful, and it was good to be back, if only for a short time.

Some people took FUBU for granted. We were a successful international brand as well as a national one. But along the way, we had moments where not everyone was feeling the love, whether it was because of the way I handled things or just because FUBU was growing fast. Let me share a few stories with you that didn't turn out the way people thought they should.

During my time at FUBU, I decided to sell my co-op apartment in Greenwich Village and move to a midtown spot that became my *Sex and the City* apartment. The elevators opened into the apartment. It was a full loft on 45th Street between 5th and 6th Ave. There are not many, if any, apartments on that street, as it is a commercial street in a highly commercial area. When I found it, I immediately fell in love.

I went to the closing with my dad because he had co-signed the co-op apartment, which I bought when I returned to the States. We were the only two Black folks in the room. The men kept speaking to my father.

I spoke up and said, "Unless he is paying the mortgage on the new place, direct all questions at me."

What should have been a quiet thought came out loud from one of the white men: "How can you afford something on 5th Ave? Those FUBU people can't pay you *that* well."

I smiled, looked at him, and said, "Since I'm the one buying and you are sitting here waiting for me to tip you at the end of this, you figure it out."

At one point, the FUBU guys and I discussed looking at a few advertising agencies to see if they could do something we weren't doing, as we created all of our advertising campaigns in-house. It happened to be a time when we were traveling a lot. (When weren't we?)

One of the manufacturing partners said, "I've been reading up on agencies. I will do the first few interviews and send the ones I think you would like for meetings when you return. I will have nothing else to do with the process."

When we returned, he had three agencies for us to meet. The first two were nice, but something was missing. The third agency never made it to the table to sit down. The front desk had them wait in the lobby; I came out to say my hellos and let them know that we were finishing a meeting and would be with them shortly. I put them in one of the showrooms to lay out their work, then came back and offered them coffee.

The lead guy followed me to the coffee machine in the lobby. The man who initially interviewed them walked by, said hello, and said, "Good luck. She is tough."

D walked out of the other meeting and came towards us at the coffee machine. I was about to introduce D when the man had the audacity to pick up the diamond FB logo D (and all four owners) wore around his neck, plopped it back on his chest, and before D could say anything, said, "Boy, they must be paying you a lot." Clearly, he did not know D was one of the owners.

I looked at D and said, "Feel free to go on about your day. This meeting is canceled."

The man was startled. "What do you mean it's canceled?"

"If you didn't do your homework and didn't know who you were meeting with, you have nothing to show us," I said.

He started getting loud and asked for the man he had originally met with. I called security to stand by. The other man (white) came out to speak to the advertising guy (white) to say, "I told you it's up to them, not me. Bye."

D left, and I made sure the team packed up and was escorted out.

We never hired an ad agency, but I think we did well without one. It's hard to capture culture if you don't understand the culture, and very few ad agencies truly understood how to authentically represent us.

Another time, I worked on an interview with a prominent news outlet. They came to the FUBU office in the Empire State Building to do the interview and were impressed with the office and the views. I had the office on lockdown for noise, as was normal when camera crews came in. We were set up in both showrooms, and this was to be an extensive interview.

The focus was on the growth of the business and the industry when, all of a sudden, the reporter asked, "Did any of you sell drugs when you were young? I heard that . . ."

Before she could continue, I said, "Please stop the interview." It went left so quickly. I looked at the reporter. I was sitting off in a corner as always, where the guys could see me but not the cameras. "What relevance does this have to the story? What are you doing?" I asked.

She said, "I'm with - - - and I can ask what I want."

I asked the guys to please go sit in the lobby while I had a conversation with the reporter. The crew looked shocked. The guys got up and left. No questions asked; they knew I would handle business.

The reporter started again: "I'm with - - -. I can ask whatever I want to."

I was clear with her. "You are in our house, and you will not turn this into a 'look at these young Black men, maybe they were drug dealers' story, because they were not, and this is not what we agreed to do. This is a business story."

She started again, "Well. I can . . ."

"Well, this is over," I said. I opened the showroom door and told the guys, "The interview is over. I will come to speak with you later."

I called security and asked them to escort the news team to the elevator as they packed up their equipment. The reporter was pissed. I looked at her and said, "I'll call the producer I worked with. You are now free to go."

She gathered her things and left. As they packed up, the crew told me they had watched stories go to the left before, but because of the station's power, they never saw anyone stop it and tell them to pack up and go. They applauded me for watching out for my clients, yet they were still in shock.

When I'm asked what it was like working at FUBU, I say it was a runaway train. There was so much going on. We were a fashion company, but I spent time in LA working with TV and film wardrobe stylists and designers. I spent time with the lawyers, ensuring our agreements had a line about marketing and public relations. I worked directly with celebrities and their teams to dress them for videos, shows, and appearances. I created events and arranged sponsorships and partnerships. I oversaw all of the press for the four owners and the brand. For every new international license that joined us, I needed to learn about what worked in that country. Horse racing, racecars, MMA fighting—I learned about it all and made sure it made sense for our brand. I was the "No, you can't do that or have that" person. If it didn't fit with our brand or our vision, we didn't agree to it.

Years later, I remain friends with people I met during my FUBU journey. Some, I still collaborate with. It's almost a badge of honor to have worked during that era; if you've come out on the other side, you know how to work!

A big part of working at FUBU was sharing my world with the guys and them sharing theirs with me. We were from different worlds—we grew up differently—but that didn't stop us from working through whatever we needed to do to make it happen. I look back now, and I feel honored to have been at the forefront with the owners. It's not often you get to walk into a new brand and help shape it into a successful company. FUBU gave me opportunities to try new things while staying true to who I was and who the guys were. Because of that, I was able to create opportunities that positioned them as trailblazers—the first in many ways as owners of a fashion company.

CHAPTER 11

Shaking Things Up

In ten years at FUBU, the one thing I never heard was, "Tone it down." I may have heard, "You know you were wrong on that, right?" But "Tone it down?" Never! If anything, if someone complained about me, it was normally someone who also annoyed the guys, and the guys would sit back and laugh. We were focused on building the brand and shaking up the industry, and I had plans for how we were going to do that. The guys had no problem shaking things up in the fashion, music, and entertainment world. We were bigger than fashion!

At the time, the (entertainment) industry was all mixed together—lifestyle brands, TV, film, music, fashion, and alcohol, a.k.a. spirit brands. It was also a time when men would cross over me to get to the founders and act like they didn't literally step on my toe or didn't feel the body they nudged out of the way, only for the guys to say, "Go speak to Leslie."

Once they did come to me, I said, "If you can't say hello as you push me out of the way, then I can't help you." Some women did the same. It was funny to see who wanted to be my "friend" to get close to the guys. A big mistake. Yes, they were my bosses, but I was and still am protective of them.

A few years into my time with FUBU, I took the guys to a school in the Bronx to speak about their lives. As with all speaking engagements, I stayed in the back. One of the guys mentioned me and pointed out how I handled the brand and all of their appearances. When it was time for a Q&A, a young girl said that she thought I had to be one of the guys' wives or girlfriends because she had never seen or heard of a woman in charge of a company.

Regardless of age, in the 1990s and early 2000s, women were still not considered to be in charge of anything, let alone a company. The industry was run by men, and only a few women had the power to cut checks. Only a handful of people, period, had the power to cut checks. I was one of them. If I shared my vision and the founders saw it, they would say, "Go make it happen." It's rare to have that kind of business and creative freedom to help build a brand.

Those who knew me in the industry called me "the fixer" or "the second real Olivia Pope," referencing the show *Scandal*. If something was going wrong in a company or with a client, I would receive the "secret call," asking for advice or inquiring about someone I knew who could quietly help fix things. I also assisted in writing the aftermath press releases when things went wrong at concerts or events. Some call it spin doctoring or crisis PR. I prefer to think of it as getting things done, being strategic, knowing when not to have a knee-jerk reaction, and moving swiftly and quietly.

I often got speaking engagements, job offers, invitations to be a judge on pitch panels, or requests to consult for other brands and individuals. Several celebrities and athletes came to me asking if I would work on their team as a consultant and handle their PR, and I helped a good friend out with her PR agency when she needed an extra hand with her celebrity clients. While still working at FUBU, I was introduced to an NBA player who was very smart and wanted to work in the front house of the NBA when he retired.

Around the same time, I received a call asking if I would be interested in handling the press and events for a luxury Hennesy Cognac launch. When I was in the Hennesy office, my new contact looked up at the wall and then looked back at me. I laughed and said, "Yes, that's me." I had no idea they had taken the ad I'd starred in and blown it up; it was an entire wall in their office. It was a full-circle moment.

Both opportunities were too good to pass up. I created K.I.M. Media LLC (Keep It Moving Media). The name came from when people would knock on my office door at FUBU, and I would say, "Do you have all of the stuff you need together? If not, keep it moving and come back."

When I went to Daymond and told him about the opportunities, his exact words were, "I don't know when you'll have the time. You work here like crazy. But go ahead if you want to add more to your plate. Just don't get so big that you leave me."

I give D credit for having the insight to see that whatever I worked on outside of the office would also benefit them. I made sure they were invited to the events I produced, and when I met people while consulting for an agency or handling a celebrity, most of them would ask, "Aren't you running with the FUBU guys as well?"

K.I.M. Media began with branding, events, and public relations. One day, I would be with the FUBU guys, and the next, I'd be in a different state with my NBA player. Steve Harvey saw me on both days in different states and just laughed. He turned to me and said, "You are one hard-working woman." All my clients were aware of each other, and the connections benefited everyone. As I write this, K.I.M. Media has just celebrated twenty-five years in business. I am proud of how I built it. I worked with clients who gave me creative freedom, and I hand-picked my staff to work, laugh, and travel with. The joy of owning your own company is that you decide who you want to work with. The business has weathered the storms and keeps on growing. Here's to the next twenty-five!

Under K.I.M., I designed and produced events all over the US and internationally. I created high-end, one-of-a-kind, luxury events with budgets up to $300,000. I was known for transforming blank spaces or photography lots in LA for the evening. It was a magical process requiring a lot of hard work, and some fantastic consultants collaborated with me.

As my company grew, I was still committed to FUBU. To add one more thing to my plate, I decided to start boxing. I was a fan of boxing and, through FUBU, collaborated with Muhammad Ali on the Muhammad Ali Collection. Lennox Lewis was one of our spokespersons, and we also worked together alongside other boxers. I felt like I was in heaven discussing boxing with them, especially with Lennox.

One day, I passed a boxing gym on my way back to the FUBU office after a meeting. When I arrived at the office, I asked my staff to look up boxing gyms. They came back with Mendez Boxing, a true Mexican Boxing gym. It was the one I had passed by four blocks from the office. The next day, I went over after my gym workout. I would always get dressed for the office at the gym, so I walked into the boxing gym with my three-inch heels on and said, "What does it take to not look like a girl? I will sign up for a month and go from there." I handed Francisco, the owner, my credit card and said, "If you open at 6:00 a.m., I'll see you after the first part of my workout, by 6:45 or 7:00 a.m." I was at the first gym by 5:00 or 5:30 a.m.

I was forty when I walked into the boxing gym; I showed up every morning after that. The FUBU crew thought I had officially lost my mind. I would train, spar, shower, put my heels on, and still beat folks into the office. One day, I was sitting at my desk and felt a pain in my side, and I couldn't think of why it would be hurting. It was the middle of the day when I realized I had taken a body shot that morning, and that's why my ribs hurt. *Oh well, keep it moving!*

Francisco later told me he had looked at the other coach the day I came in and said, "We will never see her again." The joke was on them, because not only did they see me again, but I quickly went from three to six days a week. Francisco gave me a pair of gloves, and I was hooked. He would often laugh and say, "I wish I had you at fifteen. With your skills and mouth, you could be a pro." Professional female fighters didn't make as much as the men back then; they made close to nothing.

I sparred with men because almost no women were sparring in the gym at the time. After one morning sparring session, I took my gloves off, and I had broken a nail. I looked at the guy and said, "Look, you broke my nail!"

"Your entire hand broke my face," he replied.

Yes, I said nails. I still had to show up and be an executive. I also wore full makeup in the ring with my matching gym outfits. My coaches, Francisco and Salvador, would just shake their heads at me. They knew I was serious. I was also serious about not pouring water over my head.

The first time Salvador went to do this in the corner, I looked at him and said, "If I'm knocked out, do not throw water on my hair. You *never* throw water on a Black woman's hair. I don't care what you need to do, just don't do that!"

I was so serious about boxing that when I had a job in LA for K.I.M. Media to produce a large-scale event, I made arrangements to fly Francisco there with me and train with me at one of the local boxing gyms in the early mornings before I needed to meet my staff. Flying Francisco out to train me? People *really* thought I had lost it. We had a ball and trained at a few different gyms, including Oscar del Hoya's. As soon as we walked into a gym, the coaches would always say, "I have a girl she can spar with." Francisco would always say no. He said that was the oldest trick and setup. Never spar with someone you haven't seen. Mendez Boxing was well known, and it was nice to be called Mendez Girl at our home gym and within the fighting community. During that trip, we went into one gym, and I walked out with a sponsor for my first exhibition fight.

My K.I.M. staff knew how I rolled because, before I started boxing, I was always up and in the hotel gym and ready to go by call time to shop for props, take meetings, go on site visits, and do whatever we needed to do. They loved Francisco. With him speaking Spanish at the flower market in LA, my standard discount became even bigger than expected—allowing me to add that money somewhere else in the client's budget. Everyone was happy.

It was 2005, and I had a few weeks before my first exhibition fight. Three rounds, two minutes. I knew the girl I was going to fight. I had no idea if this would be my one and only fight, so I invited everyone: the FUBU guys, friends, K.I.M. staff, and my attorney. My mom and dad wanted no part of me fighting, but my sister and nephew came from Jersey. The guy I was seeing opened his lounge for me to have an after-party, where I invited the folks from the gym, my coach, and the team that helped me get ready. When I say, "get ready," I mean I trained not only in the morning but also some evenings and weekends. I had the designer at FUBU make T-shirts for my corner guys. The T-shirts read: "Team Balls." My fighting name was Balls because at my age (forty-one now) I had to have balls to step in the ring and fight. I also had an outfit designed with "Balls" written on the back of my sports bra and the corner of my skort. I was ready. Mark edited my walk-in song from DMX. "I don't give a F*** what N*****s think." I also had my sponsored boxing shoes from Pony.

I drove Francisco and Salvador crazy, asking about my weigh-in and news conference. I was the only one who had a walk-in song, as it's not normal for exhibitions to go all out. They call names, and then you get in the ring and fight. I had the small gym packed, standing room only.

I think some people came to see me get knocked out. When you're a female boxer, your coach says, "Teach them a lesson. Do not knock them out; show your technique." My dance technique would sometimes jump into my training; when I was told to pivot, I wanted to pivot as if I were in the dance studio, not in a boxing ring. When I watch the tape back from the fight, I see I did a pirouette out of a corner instead of the pivot I was taught to do. *Oops*. I loved how my body looked while I was boxing. I was thinner than when I was dancing, but I had more muscles.

My friends said that when the other woman entered the ring first, they all exchanged glances with each other and the FUBU guys, thinking, *Uh oh, this chick is bigger and looks stronger than Leslie.* I came out to my music, hearing my coach's voice in my head. The young woman I fought was 109 lbs and shorter than I was. My long arms and legs were an advantage, and I used them. She kept coming at me, and I kept her at bay. I kept wondering why she kept trying to come under my arm when, clearly, I was not going to let her get close to me.

There are no announced winners in exhibition fights; the audience decides.

I shocked everyone. Some of my guy friends, who had boxed and competed before, were left speechless. The next day, the talk in and out of the office was all about how I could really fight. It even reached Lennox Lewis's camp that I was fighting and that I was good.

I wasn't satisfied with the trophy from the gym. I was happy, but not satisfied. I rarely took vacations, but I wanted one more challenge, and that was Ringside. Ringside is three to four days of intense competition. Each morning, you check your name to see if you are on the list to fight that day. If not, you train, watch fights, and look at the other fighters to figure out who you may get paired with. I wanted to go. The FUBU crew thought I was nuts for *finally* taking a vacation . . . and then using it to fight.

Francisco and I started training for the event. I would be the first boxer to go to the competition representing Mendez Boxing, and I had no idea what I was walking into. Francisco and I flew out to Kansas City. He trained me hard, and we waited for a fight. I was in an older category, and I'd be lucky if I got one. I walked away with a belt, the first won for Mendez Boxing.

FUBU and the other male fighters at the ring had to sit back when I showed up in the office with the belt. If you have been on Zoom with me, you have seen that belt behind me. It sits across from a bronzed pointe shoe that was given to me as a gift after I performed a ballet created for me.

I retired from fighting after winning the belt, but I obtained my coaching license and helped train fighters at the gym. Whenever I showed up for fights and entered the locker room, if anyone looked at me sideways, people would say, "That's Mendez's girl," and the looks would vanish.

Francisco passed away from COVID in 2020. My heart broke when I heard the news. His son, whom I remember as a child, discovered pictures of his dad and me from the LA trip, Kansas City, and so many other adventures. He brought them to the gym and asked, "Who is this? I sort of remember." Salvador, my other coach, shared stories of his dad and me, while his mother filled in details. I'm happy to say that with the gym closing during COVID, Francisco's son later opened a successful gym, and we still keep in touch. I'm always in awe of how Francisco took me under his wing and believed in my potential for a pro career. He will always live in my heart.

In 2008, with K.I.M. Media growing, I decided it was time. I had been at FUBU for ten years, and I didn't feel like I could give it anymore. It was time to bring in new blood with new thoughts. I let Daymond know first. He ignored me. I told him I wouldn't leave until there was a replacement.

A friend of mine, who was the CEO of a bank, could not believe I would give up an executive salary and a corner office.

He kept saying, "Don't you know people work their entire lives to get what you have?"

"I had it. Now it's time to move on," I answered.

I did have the best of both worlds: an executive salary and what I was creating at K.I.M. But for me, it wasn't about the salary. If I was growing without hardly trying, what could I do with K.I.M. if I focused? D and I finally agreed, but I think everyone else still thought I was joking. During my ten years, there had been many times that I'd yelled, "I'm quitting," or, "I'm not speaking to you," so folks thought I wasn't really going to leave. I also had the hardest time finding a replacement. I thought a few people would jump at the chance to have creative freedom and work with the FUBU founders. Instead, people who were already in the industry said no. They knew they would be compared to what I had accomplished; I spoiled the guys, and they were expecting a lot because I gave a lot. I kept hearing, "No, thank you, hard pass." It took longer than the month I expected to stay after giving my notice.

I finally found someone interested, and it happened to be a girl from the gym, a boxer. I was able to make the transition. Notice how I didn't say I left! After ten years, I left the office as an employee on a Friday and was back the following Monday as a consultant to finish closing a project I had worked on. Ever since, FUBU has been a client of K.I.M. Media on a consultant basis as needed. Twenty-something years later, we remain intertwined.

Once I stopped offering PR at K.I.M. Media, I had fun creating, designing, and producing events. I also consulted on branding and marketing for various companies, overseeing their luxury and international brands. I was still getting calls to work on all types of products in all types of fields.

When the market crashed in 2008 and companies pulled back from high-end events, it was tough for a moment. Even the magazines were folding. I kept working. Everyone knew I produced luxury events and had an entire team, which meant I was expensive to hire. However, I did not have a full team; I had consultants I would call when needed. I mainly worked with the same crew, so I appeared to be larger than I was even without the cost of a whole staff. This helped me stay afloat.

When I came back from the LA event where we had created flower designs, I started looking for vendors in the flower market in New York. Everyone was on one main street, along with the shops selling vases and smaller props. I walked into a few flower shops, and I was ignored. Maybe the salespeople thought I had a small budget; I'm Black, and they didn't know me, so they took care of the folks they did know. Still, they couldn't even be bothered to see what I wanted. I walked into one shop where there was one person ahead of me. The man working looked at me and said, "Give me five. You are next."

After that, I worked with Chris for every event. I even had him ship to me in Aspen for my Food and Wine events. Chris was the only one who didn't think twice about not knowing me or my client list. When the industry slowed down, I kept working with my Asian clients, creating curated dinners. I went to wherever Chris was working, and that's where my large floral budget went. I recall a day when the vendors were standing in their doorways, and they asked me if they could help me source an item. I just laughed. Too little, too late. "No, thanks." I went to Chris.

Very few Black women and a handful of Black men designers worked with flowers, let alone produced events, when I was getting started with K.I.M. Therefore, vendors would assume we didn't have large clients with large budgets. After an event, one caterer confessed to me that he'd told his staff he didn't think I would show up with the $35,000 deposit for the food and bar. Yes, he said it was because I was Black.

I had the opportunity to produce an event for the African TV Network, setting up the room for the cocktails and creating the flowers for the dinner table and stage. One of the older Black servers told me he was surprised to see me. I was only the second Black event or flower designer to have produced any type of event at that hotel. The first was a well-known event designer, and I was the first Black female designer. The server had worked in the hotel for over thirty years and worked the banquets. He told me he was proud to see me and hoped I would be back.

On the other side of town, I worked with Rémy Martin for their high-end Asian consumer events. Understanding Europe and Asia has been and continues to be what makes my firm different. I traveled around the country, curating dinners and producing events, launching high-end spirits for several companies with a focus on their Asian markets and luxury markets. At one launch, the key clients introduced me to their guests as their "Asian expert." The guests looked at each other and smiled; they were Asian.

As we sat in a meeting preparing for a tour, one of the Asian marketing staff at Rémy Martin joined the meeting and asked, "Why is the urban agency here? This is for our market."

Before I could say anything, the Senior Account Director stated, "Leslie's agency will be handling the tour. Please be prepared to respond when and if she needs you."

I guess I was the "urban agency" because I'm Black.

K.I.M. Media was busier than ever when we were approached to produce a large luxury spirit product launch event. The French office originally wanted a French agency to handle it, but the New York office wanted my firm to handle it. In another full-circle moment, David LaChapelle was part of the project and remembered me from the ad he had shot with me for Hennessy years before. There was a lot riding on this product launch, and the French office was very involved. It helped that, as bad as my French is, I could understand and speak enough to understand when they were not happy or speaking about someone in the meeting. The French office thought we should share the project between agencies, but the French agency had never produced an event in the US for a mixed cultural influencer market (way before making money as an influencer was a thing). Plus, the event was in LA. People are different out there.

The French office hated long presentations, and the US marketing team had put one together. "Leslie, tell them no," the French team said.

Oh, now I'm part of the French office? I thought.

The American office asked me to explain how things worked, and there I was again, the liaison between France and America.

We all flew out to LA for site visits; I selected venues, as did the French agency. We spent two days at sites and did not reach an agreement. The French concept was to build a rotating box where guests would step inside as the lights changed colors—that was the "big idea." But in LA, asking people to stand in a spinning box didn't resonate; it wasn't connecting with the spirit of the launch. I decided everyone was fighting too hard and losing sight of the amazing artwork. The artwork that David LaChapelle had created for the bottle was vibrant, colorful, and told a story. I expressed my desire to take over a photography studio, which would be a blank canvas to bring the bottle to life. Every hour would represent a color from the bottle. The food, waitstaff attire, drinks, music, and the entire room would change color every hour. During the second hour, the woman from the bottle would come alive through dance, yet the party would never stop. The event concept was all about the senses, which was also part of the marketing plan. Everyone agreed. I worked with skilled vendors and built an exotic jungle as part of the red carpet and cocktail hour.

In LA, it's easy to create and source props and live foliage. I tracked down the lighting company that had just worked on the GRAMMYs. They had debuted a standing bulb that I wanted as part of the DJ stage, which I envisioned in the sky. Once we met, we knew we would work together. They were creative, and the owner and I hit it off, bouncing with ideas about how the lighting and design would flow. When the crew came to load in two days before the event, one of the guys looked at me and said, "I don't know what you did to the owner, but you have more gear than the Mick Jagger concert we just lit."

I rented the venue for a week for a one-night event. We needed to build the set and then have time to break it down. The event was phenomenal. I knew changes would be coming, as that's part of the industry: Never get comfortable with a client, and always stay on your creative toes! But I was incredibly proud of what we'd accomplished.

The best part about K.I.M. Media is that I am still friends with so many of my clients. We worked that closely together. When I would go on site visits with clients, the contacts at the venues were always surprised that I would lead the meeting and direct my client on how I thought everything should be presented and flow. My clients never pushed back.

After one meeting, the venue contact came to me and said, "I've never seen an agency work with their client in that way."

I just smiled and said, "It works for us."

I knew that I had my clients' trust to make the best decision for them and to make sure they looked good for their bosses and for the brand. We shared a lot of laughs, traveling for events and working on projects. They always knew that whatever I presented to them would shake things up for the brand—in the right way.

CHAPTER 12

God Has a Plan—Or, Never Say Never

I have always said that K.I.M. Media does not do weddings. When I received requests to design or handle a wedding, I would say no thanks. It's just not my thing. I loved creating transformational events, though. They were always a welcomed challenge.

Then, in 2010, my close friend proposed to his girlfriend. "I want you to do the wedding," he said to me.

"One, I don't do weddings," I responded. "And two, typically, the woman decides whom she wants to work with."

"Will you at least take the meeting?" he asked.

I knew his fiancée, but I didn't know her well. I agreed to meet and share the knowledge and connections I had about venues—whatever they needed. However, I still didn't do weddings. After several meetings and site visits, they asked me again to please handle the wedding. They said there would be many moving parts, which they couldn't entrust to someone unless they knew the person could handle it. I finally agreed to produce and design the wedding but said they needed to hire a coordinator to handle the wedding stuff.

I started asking others in the industry about people they knew who worked like me but did weddings. They sent me a few names, but most people simply shook their heads, saying, "Wedding planners are different." We decided on a planner and made it clear that there would be deep cultural meanings throughout, as the wedding was being held at the oldest Black Baptist church in the US. I asked if the planner had a multicultural staff, as it would be necessary for a smooth event, especially with this venue. The planner told me they did, but the night of the wedding rehearsal at the church, there was not a single person of color on that team. That was going to be an issue, because there were cultural needs we couldn't teach overnight after many months of planning and meetings.

I called in a favor from someone I knew who had previously worked on weddings. She came in and saved the day, as the church elders listened to her. We made it through the ceremony, then I ran to the next location to check on that setup and staff. I had staff in four different locations throughout the day and evening, plus the wedding planner's team. How things went wrong, I still don't know. I do know my staff needed to jump in to help with the wedding planner's parts, even after all the months of meetings, walkthroughs, and my famous sixty-page production books that detailed every move of every person, object, and delivery, along with anything that needed to happen with anyone involved in the ceremony or the two receptions.

By the time the evening was over, I was pissed at the number of visible mistakes that my clients saw. I returned to my loft, where several staff were spending the night. As we did after every event, we opened wine, pulled out the cheese, talked about the night, laughed at stuff that happened, and discussed what we could do better next time. I didn't do weddings until that night; that was when K.I.M. Weddings was born—out of sheer frustration.

"It can't be that hard; it's not brain surgery," I said. I decided I would jump in and do weddings my way.

In the midst of working on that wedding and my regular events, I lost a very good friend. Dana, the young music artist I danced for in France, died of cancer at age thirty-two. She had become like my little sister, so when her mother called and asked me to dress her, I didn't hesitate. I had dressed her on stage and for her marriage, and now I had the honor to dress her at death.

The morning she passed, I ran around calling my fashion friends and stopping into stores, trying to find something to cover her neck. The after-death surgical procedure leaves scars on the neck, but anything I could find to cover it made her look like an old lady. I kept saying, "We needed to make scarves and items for young people at the time of death. Why should death be focused on the elderly?"

My friends kept saying, "Stop trying to build a new business and focus on your friend."

But something was wrong with how the business was being handled. The family spoke to more than one funeral director due to scheduling issues, and the night before the funeral, the older director told them that her full name wouldn't fit on the plaque.

I looked at the family and asked, "May I handle this?"

They were happy to turn it over to me. I had helped where I could throughout the process, but it wasn't my place to jump in and take over until her mother looked at me that night and said,

"Please do what you do, Leslie."

I took the older funeral director into the back room and asked him to change the point size and the font size of my friend's name to make sure it would fit.

He looked at me and said, "Miss, I have no idea what you are talking about."

I asked him to call the vendor, and I spoke directly with the vendor to make it happen. Then I came back out to the family to say it was taken care of, and so was her outfit. That was a bit harder due to her size and wanting to project her style. When Dana came back to the US, one of her internships was with a high-end designer. When the designer heard she had passed, she offered to provide one of Dana's favorite dresses she had admired in the showroom.

Dana's death altered my life. I am still honored to have been asked not only to dress her at the time of her passing, but also to manage those family matters. Working the one-day, four-venue wedding, especially with many guests being part of the ministry, also shifted the direction of my life. The guests knew I had lost a friend during the planning process, and they understood I was very dissatisfied with how funerals were typically handled.

"There must be a better way," I kept insisting. Why isn't that being done? Why was it done this way?"

They kept responding with suggestions to attend seminary.

"But why do I need to go to seminary?" I questioned. "I want to disrupt the funeral industry." First, I wanted to create fashionable dickies . Dickies are fake collars that make it look like you're wearing a full shirt, blouse, or sweater. If you're not sure what a dickie is, Google "dickies collars."

"Why can't we make dickies look good?" I kept asking. "The fashion industry has plenty of fabric scraps being tossed away."

They would reply with seminary every time. No matter what I said, their answer was always seminary.

I started calling those same friends who pushed or "guided" me to speak more about death and dying in their ministry. I called a Rabbi, I called an ex-monk, and I talked to my Muslim friends, my friends who didn't believe in anything, a good friend who was a Jehovah's Witness, and my Buddhist friends. I wanted to understand how different cultures and religions thought about death and dying. Those are two separate topics, and my conversations focused on both.

After several lengthy discussions, I agreed to explore a certificate program. Somehow, that exploration led me to enroll in Saturday classes for two years to earn a certificate in Pastoral Care. The course was designed for busy people who wanted to know about pastoral care and become more active in their church. I ordered all of the books, and I was a nervous wreck. I was not a Bible-toting, "I can quote every verse" kind of person. I was someone who had always known God would be the foundation of her life, and that's how I moved through this world. I wasn't sure if that would help me when it was time to take tests.

For a class filled with people wanting to learn about pastoral care, they liked to bully me a bit, making a point of calling me the teacher's pet. It wasn't that I was getting A's on all my papers; it was that I asked questions and wanted to know more than what I was getting. The professors liked that I challenged myself and them.

I would read the next chapter on my way home on the train to stay a step ahead. I was fully committed, but I was disappointed that there was only one elective workshop on death and dying. I took it, and it happened to be a weekend retreat. I managed to get the teacher alone to ask about additional books I could read. I explained my desire to build a business, and she told me it was possible, but that it would be tough. I laughed. She did not know who she was speaking to.

Why are we teaching people to preach, but not how to support others during their time of need? I wondered. *Why the lack of compassion?* I decided to create my own path, realizing seminary wasn't for me. I scheduled an appointment with my advisor to inform her that my focus wasn't on preaching and that I needed a different route to achieve my goals. She began asking me questions about what it was I wanted to do. I explained that I wanted to ensure I had the knowledge to build out my business idea, which would involve working with churches, families, funeral homes, and grave sites. My assistance would depend on clients' requests. My advisor asked if I would meet with the dean.

We walked to the dean's office, where several students were waiting to speak with her. What did I have to lose at this point? The dean asked if I would consider joining the master's program. I laughed and replied that I didn't have a college degree. I had taken law and human rights classes, and I possessed several certifications, but no degree. She stated that my life experiences exceeded the requirements of a college degree. She wanted to personally place me in the program. I didn't have time to think; all I heard was that I would be challenged and, from what I understood, I would challenge them in return. Before I knew it, I was handing over my credit card and enrolling in the pastoral care master's program.

It was a challenge. The first semester, I took two classes at night after work. I was always the one raising my hand to point out that the syllabus and the required reading or assignments did not match. I didn't have the luxury of figuring it out. I was running a company, and this was not my next step after graduating from college. One professor seemed annoyed when I would respond to his question with one of my own. I stayed after class to speak to him. He laughed and then went on to tell me how he was not annoyed, but that now, he thought other students would also press for different answers and challenge him.

I made it through my classes and focused all of my papers on death and dying. A professor told me to keep every paper, as that would make it easy for me to create my dissertation. I went to speak to the nuns in the Catholic bookshop as part of my research. They did not want to speak to me at first, but I stayed until someone finally came to answer my questions. In my head, I thought, *Sisters, I have nothing but time, and I need this information for my paper. I'm not leaving. Yes, I will buy something, but I am not leaving until one of you takes the time to speak to me.* I received the information I needed.

I made sure every page of that paper was numbered and every footnote noted. I went beyond the required fifteen pages to ensure I was clear and that my argument on the topic was backed up by facts. After Thanksgiving, I turned my paper in. But I thought long and hard about the next set of courses, which were not focused on taking care of people, but on preaching. I had taken the preaching class; I had gone on the death and dying retreat again. I went back to the dean and thanked her. I said, "I need to do this my way. I will be leaving the program."

I kept studying. I found a woman who taught clergy about death and dying and bereavement, but she told me that, unfortunately, she did not have enough people to sign up for the next workshop. I told her I would pay her for private classes. The private class was what I got, and I had the opportunity to ask as many questions as I wanted; it was amazing.

As I read and took additional courses, I had no desire to pray with people. I had always said I didn't pray out loud. (Watch what you keep telling yourself you don't do!) I learned about a free course at the local hospital that offered pastoral care classes and a certificate. I never thought about the hospital, except that I was the friend you called when you were in the hospital and things weren't going right. *I want to take care of people at the time of death, but I need to understand what families are going through as part of the dying process in the hospital,* I thought. The course seemed like it would be a great way to learn, and it was free.

Father O'Leary, the hospital chaplain, taught the pastoral care class. I enjoyed it, except for the praying out loud part, but I got over that. Four weeks into the class, the time came for us to be assigned hospital floors to visit patients. We needed to remember what the patients said, but we could not take notes in front of them. Father O'Leary reminded us that not every patient wants prayer. Sometimes, they want company, and sometimes, they try to use us to get around the nurses and hospital rules. We would need to keep our ears, eyes, and hearts open. I loved this assignment!

Each patient was aware that we were there to learn and that we would need to report back; they had agreed to be part of the program. When I shared one of my conversations with Father O'Leary, he was surprised. He told me he had seen that patient for the last week; she had never shared with him what she shared with me. He pulled me aside after class to let me know he would be announcing that the hospital needed pastoral care volunteers, and he thought I would be a good fit. After completing the certificate program, I applied and was accepted as a pastoral care volunteer.

I started going to the hospital after church on Sundays. I would typically conduct visits for two hours, as well as volunteer for Palm Sunday or other holidays. I loved the hospital on Sundays. It was fairly quiet, and doctors weren't running in and out every fifteen minutes, so patients were usually a bit more settled. Those who went to some type of religious service on the weekends were sad to miss it and would be waiting for visits from their congregation or happy to have someone else visit. A hospital is a place that not only heals your body, but also makes you take stock of your life and how you are living. Some patients are grateful; others have regrets, and when they lie in that hospital bed without the world's distractions, their head can be a scary place.

Father O'Leary did not work on the weekends, and there were times he needed help during the week. I lived a fifteen-minute walk from the hospital and worked for myself, so I would jump in and help whenever I could. Who knew I would enjoy being at the hospital as much as I did? I saw births, deaths, burns, and near deaths. When I knocked on the door and said, "pastoral care volunteer," some patients were quick to throw off the sheet and show me something. I would have to state, "No, sorry, I am not a doctor. I'm here to share a prayer or a blessing if you would like one." I learned that many people would say, "I'll take a blessing, not a prayer. I'm not worthy of prayer." I learned to say "blessings or prayers" because I wanted people to feel that they were worthy of having someone focused on them and their healing, however they wanted to receive it.

Word got back to Father O'Leary that the Sunday volunteer was doing great work and that patients were asking for me. He gave me a call and said, "I don't know what you are doing, but I keep hearing wonderful things about you. And it's crazy, because the hospital executives are not working on Sunday, yet they are speaking about you as well." I was pleased only because I enjoyed doing something bigger than myself. I would pray before I walked into the hospital that God would guide me and give me the correct words and spirit for each person.

Being at the hospital, even as a volunteer, allowed me to understand family dynamics, how clergy handled hospital visits, and the complexities of social work, rehab centers, hospice, and insurance. I now had the knowledge to help families from A to Z, and I could call on people who had worked in the field for years. Just because I wasn't Jewish didn't mean I couldn't help someone Jewish when they came to the hospital, either. I would ask if they wanted me to call their Rabbi or the hospital Rabbi. I let the family know where they could rest and receive kosher food and snacks. I helped when someone at the hospital didn't understand why a family member wouldn't open the electric door on Saturday, and so many other cultural norms. The same was true for Muslim patients. I could get them a Quran as quickly as I could bring a Bible or a Rosary to someone's bedside. Sick is sick; my job was to show grace.

I started Ascend Bereavement Management (ABM) to manage business for families at the time of a loved one's death. I assisted with arrangements and acted as the liaison for the church, funeral home, grave site, restaurant, repass, and clothing. I ensured everything remained organized and peaceful within the family. Initially, some funeral homes were unhappy to see me because they thought I was taking their jobs. However, once they realized I ensured that payments were made promptly, clothes arrived on time, and answers were provided, they recognized I was an added value, not just another hand in the pot.

Meanwhile, I was still busy with K.I.M. Media, and K.I.M. Weddings was in full swing. I had built it the way I wanted to work. I was known for cultural weddings—Jewish, Indian, African, LGBTQ+, traditional, and religious. I focused on bringing culture and cultural relevance to the weddings I designed. Some were traditional, but I always made sure it was about the couple and their personality. I interviewed couples the way they interviewed me. I only wanted to work with good people, and I was able to do that. At one point, I had to pull back on weddings because they were starting to take over my consulting and event business. Not a bad problem to have. I would miss a few Sundays when I needed to travel for weddings, but I always stayed attached to the hospital.

One day, I was in my office when I received a call from Father O'Leary. He would be retiring, and the person who was supposed to replace him could not start for four weeks. Would I be interested in taking over as interim chaplain of the hospital? I almost fell off my chair. I don't surprise that easily, but I was shocked. I kept responding, "What, me? Why me? There are so many other more qualified people."

Turns out, my name had come up from the executive office and others on the hiring committee. I was given the schedule and told what was expected of me. The committee explained how I would use the system as an interim chaplain. I still needed to do the paperwork to be an employee, but I would only work for three hours per day, five days a week.

The process moved quickly because Father O'Leary was leaving in a week to return to Ireland. While this was going on, I was working and consulting again with Daymond for his new company while also taking chaplain classes to be part of the New York State Chaplains Task Force. When Rev. Marcos, who ran the organization, had heard I was the one replacing Father O'Leary, if only in an interim position, he said he wanted me to be part of the trainer program. So, I was in class *and* learning to teach others who wanted to take the class in the future to become a community chaplain.

I laughed and spoke to God. I always joked, "You wouldn't let me come to work for you when I was younger and wanted to be a 'fashionable nun' with accessories. You gave me the talent to dance, and you did call me later." I felt humbled by the experience I was having in ministry.

Before becoming interim chaplain, I didn't visit the children's floor or the NICU ward. Within the first hour of my first day as interim chaplain, my beeper went off; it was the fifth floor. My heart sank. I needed to gather myself, pray, and let God know I saw he had jokes.

I arrived on the fifth floor. "Who are you?" the nurse said.

"I am Chaplain Short, the interim chaplain. How may I help?" I answered.

"We lost a baby, and the mother wants prayer for herself and the baby before we remove it."

I approached the room, and I took a deep breath before I knocked. All the lights were off, and the mother was rightfully distraught, as was her mother. I told them that I was the chaplain, gave my condolences, and just listened to them share with me. I said nothing, allowing them to speak and cry, and afterwards they thanked me for just listening. I took their hands with their permission and prayed. The mother asked if I would pray over the baby. I did so silently and out loud, then said my goodbyes. The first thing you learn as a chaplain is never to promise you will be back. Things change, schedules change, and you don't want a patient waiting on you. I didn't know if I would see the family again, but I knew my time with them would stay with me.

That visit to the fifth floor may have been my first, but it was not my last. One of the other stories that will stay with me was a month into the interim position, when I was called to the fifth floor again. A couple had lost their baby just before they could have footprints and hair taken. Both would be difficult to do because of the size of the fetus and the hospital policy on how that was handled.

It was their first pregnancy. I could never answer "why" questions. Even when people asked me, "Why did God—?" I was honest: "I don't know. Here is what I do know . . ." This couple told me they had asked for footprints and hair—the smallest way to keep a piece of their lost child with them—and asked me if I would ask the nurses again. That was a request I had no problem fulfilling. When I went to the nurses' station and asked again, they all just looked at each other.

"What's going on?" I asked.

"Well, the fetus was at the cusp, so it is in the refrigerator to go to the morgue," they said.

"So, what I'm hearing is the baby was on the cusp, it's still on this floor, and getting the footprint and the hair is possible. If that's the case, it should happen for the couple."

"It's already in the solution in the fridge," the nurse said.

Louder than I intended, I stated, "This couple thought they would leave this hospital in a few months with a baby. Today, they will leave with nothing other than paperwork on how to retrieve the fetus from the morgue. The *least* they could have is footprints and a lock of hair. *I'll* do it."

Now, to this very day many years later, I have no idea why I said I would go remove the fetus from the fridge and make it happen myself. That was God speaking, not me! Meanwhile, the head nurse was on the phone, and the nurse was telling her, "The chaplain said she would do it."

I heard a loud, "*No*! That's not her job. It's yours. *Go*!"

The two nurses were shaking. I stopped them and said, "I will go with you."

I prayed with them before they went in. They came back out with the footprints but no hair. They explained that there was very little hair before and none now.

I understood, hugged them, and said, "You have done something very special today."

I went back to the couple and handed them the footprints. The father broke down, and all they could both say was "thank you." It wasn't about a prayer. It was about advocating for them—the Ministry of Presence.

Four weeks turned into six months of working as the interim chaplain. I think they forgot I was not there permanently. It wasn't like they didn't see me; I turned in my reports. I didn't need to attend all of the meetings because I was only there for three hours a day. If a holiday fell during the week, I was there. I would still pop in sometimes on Sundays, as I missed seeing that staff of nurses and doctors.

While working at the hospital, I helped run the bereavement group for families, patients, and hospital staff. I also created a support group for patients with sickle cell anemia, a disease that predominantly affects African Americans and people of color. Those patients know the hospital and the system better than the doctors and nurses, which opens them up to being taken for granted. Sickle cell is a painful disease. I watched several patients and their families come in and out of the hospital, sometimes on the main floors, and other times in the ICU. I noticed that once the patients turned eighteen, they were left to fend for themselves, with no programs and no help. They came in and out, and the drugs they got in the hospital were a different strength than what they got at home. Some went from hospital to hospital seeking drugs; many of them just wanted relief, and some had other issues as well.

I got to know these patients and asked for permission to start a group. I asked the nurses if I could move their patients to the lounge area I secured on the next floor. Then, I went to the rehab room and asked to borrow a wheelchair or two if needed. I told each patient when to be up and ready to bring the notebooks I bought for them. Some of the nurses were just happy to have a break from having the patients on their floor, as a few of them could be demanding or combative with the nurses—I would sometimes get a call to please come help calm them down. The group lasted as long as I did. It cost me nothing but time; I used the money people left in the chapel to buy notebooks for the patients to draw or write. I was sad that other people in the hospital didn't see the value in the group. I asked one of the doctors if it was because they were Black and brown, and he said, "Yes. Deep down, yes."

As I prepared to leave the hospital, several doctors I spoke with asked if I was a mediator. I had no idea what that meant outside of the hospital context. They all suggested I look into it. "You are the chaplain, but we call you for everything concerning family issues," one doctor explained. "You have a talent for calming people and translating our language for their understanding. You should be a mediator; you already are one."

I researched what mediating entailed. In general, mediation is a process where parties in conflict meet with a neutral third party who helps them negotiate through their differences. There are also forms of mediation designed to help people navigate difficult family situations. I found a course in Boston that would perfectly suit ABM. The course focused on elder, adult, and family mediation.

Before I could take the course in Boston, I needed to take the basic mediation class—no exceptions, no way around it. God again stepped in, and I found a class in the Bronx that was about to begin, which finished just before I needed to leave for Boston. Today, I am a certified mediator. The knowledge I gained has benefited me in the mediation field and every career path I have chosen. It equips me with additional tools that other agencies lack.

Being the chaplain at the hospital was by far the most important thing I have accomplished. Leaving the hospital was not the end of my chaplaincy. I taught chaplain classes, preached for clergy anniversaries, and even delivered a sermon at the Catholic church. After the sermon, I sat in the back with the priest. "See, I didn't take you to 'Black Church,'" I joked.

"No," he said, "but you did add a shoulder roll or two, and I loved it."

I am a minister and have performed weddings and funerals, but I prefer to call myself a chaplain, because I care for everyone. Regardless of what you may think of me, if you are human and need support, I will be there for you. I will put on my chaplain's hat and, without judgment, ensure that I help you get to where you need to be, whether the road is long or short. And if I'm not the best fit for you, I will make sure to connect you with someone who can continue the journey alongside you.

Chaplaincy gave me what I was looking for within ministry: a way to serve in a meaningful way. I believe it has impacted the way I conduct my workshops, hold meetings, and run my business. Yes, I'm still tough, and I expect a lot. Some will say I am mean; I say I am direct. But whatever words are used to describe me, I hope that, if you were in a situation where you needed help, I showed you grace. Chaplaincy taught me how to give grace and accept it as I listen to my spirit and move how it leads me in business, life, and love.

CHAPTER 13

Expanding Beyond the Current Culture

In 2017, after my interim chaplain position came to an end, I was invited to visit Israel for an educational seminar for community leaders. It was a fantastic trip and I learned a great deal, though I walked away saying it was very complicated. Just because I enjoyed the trip doesn't mean I agreed with everything the government was doing. (I don't agree with everything the French or American government does either.) The trip opened conversation, understanding, and confusion all at the same time. It allowed me to have more sensitivity towards countries in the region, each with its own pain points that are beyond what I can fix, but with which I can recognize and sympathize. Visiting the region, I also saw how, regardless of religion or politics, people want love, safety for their families, food, shelter, and health care—things no one should be denied, especially not because of religion or politics.

I spent the year meeting with people from all fields and looking at issues in the workplace. I went to Columbia University and took a Human Rights course. I wasn't sure if I wanted to work in human rights or Diversity, Equity, and Inclusion. I felt that human rights were presented in two parts: In one, the corporate world makes it happen, but you stay in the office, and others do the work on the ground. In the other, you do the work on the ground, and the conditions are what they are. I didn't want to just approve what was going to get done; I wanted some type of hands-on experience. I decided there was a way I could work in human rights in whatever direction I chose.

In my work and studies, I was able to discuss work, gender, race, religion, and language. If you remember, I had already managed multicultural marketing and was typically the one advocating for individuals in the workplace, whether it was a dance studio or an office building. The international discussions, in contrast to the American conversations, thrilled me. I started to concentrate on what Diversity, Equity, and Inclusion signified in the US *and* abroad. The recurring question for me was, "Why is DEI so difficult for people to understand?"

During that time, I was also considering whether I should work for someone else and let them pay my health insurance. K.I.M. Media was doing okay, but I wanted to design fewer events. ABM was more of a ministry organization. I typically got paid when I worked, but it was based on what a family could afford. ABM wasn't focused on making money, but rather on being of service. If I were to discuss workplace culture and DEI, it would require a different company.

I held a full week of meetings discussing in-house opportunities since I had no desire to start another company. I attended informational meetings and connected with friends, and everyone had someone for me to meet. I left every meeting feeling frustrated by the lack of culture and the complaints coming from senior-level employees.

During one meeting, an older white man said, "Leslie, you're kidding yourself if you think anyone is going to hire you for an in-house position."

"Why?" I asked, half-laughing.

"Are you serious? The old white guys like me are scared you're going to come in, take one look around, and say, 'This is a mess. Let me fix this,' and then we'll be out of a job. Plus, you're too expensive to bring in. But I'll pay you to advise me."

At my meeting the next day, someone said, "Figuring out how to hire senior-level people of color is hard."

"How is it hard?" I asked.

"I don't know where to look."

"Okay, but we are in New York. Where did you look?"

Blank stare.

"Exactly," I said. "You want to talk about it but not do the work."

Next meeting, same day: "Great conversation, Leslie. What's the name of your firm? I have work for you if you decide to do this; what you just said is what I need, and it makes sense."

I went home that day, moved the rest of my meetings that week, and sat on my sofa. Folks had made me angry. And what happens when I'm pissed? I build it. I started to map out what I was going to call this new agency. I considered how I would build this company differently from what was currently in the market. *This is bigger than initials*, I thought. *This is culture, and companies just assume that if they open the doors, people will come and work. It's a different time.*

Time was on my side to build the company the way I wanted it. I didn't want to rush into opening the doors until I had several pieces in place. First, I wanted three different councils: Advisor, Inclusion, and Executive. Each council and council member would bring something different to the table. I'd need people working in various fields—champions, advocates, and allies of building culture and inclusive workplaces.

Next, I needed to come up with a name. I knew I did not want it to have "diversity and inclusion" as part of the name because it was much bigger than that; names can limit you. I wanted the company to have a name that would make people ask, "What does it mean?" When President Bush Sr. passed, some news segments spoke about his aviation career. I was watching a special on his life while writing down and googling names when I heard the word "Cavu," an aviation term used by pilots to declare Ceiling and Visibility Unlimited—in other words, a perfect day for flying.

I jumped up and said, "That's it! I have the name! The Cavu Group."

I did research and saw that the name was not being used in my field. I called my lawyer; I needed to tell him that, one, I was starting a business, and two, could we make it a DBA? (DBA stands for "doing business as," and lets people know that a business entity is operating under a different name than registered.) I decided to make The Cavu Group a DBA of K.I.M. Media LLC, because that business had an established reputation. I could get The Cavu Group up and running faster that way.

I had told someone that I was building the company, and they hired me before I even finished the site or logo design. What they wanted me to handle didn't start for a few months, so I had a little time. I already felt I was on to something; I just needed to wrap my head around how to present it to others beyond the people I knew. This was not going to be a traditional agency that just offered workshops. I would bring my other skills—mediation, conflict coaching, and leadership—into play.

A week or so after finding a name for The Cavu Group, I caught up with a good friend and told her what I was building. "I'm in," she stated.

"What do you mean you're in?" I asked.

"Whatever you're building, I know I want in," she replied.

I laughed it off, but a few weeks later, once I had a better idea of how we could work together, I called her back and said, "Are you serious?" I shared some additional thoughts.

"I'm in," she repeated, "and here's how I can help."

Around the same time, I caught up with another good friend for lunch and told him about the business. He looked at me and asked if I had secured all of the social media platforms with the name. I said I had not. I just decided on the name a few days ago. He didn't care. He snatched my phone, locked down all the social media platforms with the company name, and immediately started discussing logos with me.

I knew the colors I desired, and I knew I wanted a clean logo, one symbol or letter that would allow me not to use the full name all the time. The C was exactly it. My friend wanted time to play around with the blue colors; he also agreed to help build the website. Everything was falling into place, including speaking with the people I wanted to have on the councils. By the time we were ready to sign contracts, The Cavu Group was up and running. My focus and tagline—and my belief—is that you have to "Expand Beyond Your Current Culture."

I started The Cavu Group the same way I started K.I.M. Media—with clients. Soon after we launched, I was invited to a cocktail with an organization that knew me well. I was speaking to one of the directors about the business, and he said, "Why would you open a firm about diversity, inclusion, and company culture? That doesn't make sense, plus there are so many of them."

"Name two and tell me what they do or who runs them," I said.

Crickets.

A year later, that very company would hire me to handle culture.

Within a year of launching The Cavu Group, I was asked to be a keynote speaker on culture and workplace behaviors at an executive conference in DC. At first, I wasn't thrilled, because it was not a paid gig. However, expenses would be taken care of, and I was already in DC for a different conference. I could jump in a car and be at the other venue for two days without too much fuss. I also found out there would be three keynote speakers; I was one, and one of the others was the President of Ben & Jerry's Ice Cream. No one was getting paid, and the room was full of corporations. It would be an excellent opportunity to speak about The Cavu Group. Not only did I give a keynote, but I also sat on a panel and ran a thought leader group. I learned that sometimes, when you are starting something new, even if you have a reputation and a history, you may need to reintroduce yourself to a new generation of people. That's exactly what I did.

The morning of my keynote, I came down to grab a bite, listen to the first speaker, and scout out the room. There were vendor tables set up, and I went to browse and see what was going on. I looked at a book publisher's display with various business books on his table, but the man did not seem very friendly, and I walked away. When I circled back around, something told me to go back to the table. I asked him if he had a book on diversity, inclusion, and company culture.

He looked up and said, "No, I have authors who have written a chapter or two, but nothing dedicated to that. I would be interested."

Wait, what? Interesting. We spoke for a bit, I snuck in to watch a bit more of the keynote, then passed by the table again and said, "I'm the keynote after lunch. If you have a moment, pop in."

He handed me his card and said, "Get in touch."

I decided to send him an email after that conference, and we set up a call. I explained that I had worked on books with celebrities and had received a book offer in the past. I wasn't trying to be rich or famous; I understood it could be a great marketing tool. I also explained how I looked at company culture through the lens of diversity and inclusion.

At the end of the call, he said, "If you like, I'd like to do your book. I'll send you a contract. Look it over, and let's do this."

It amused me how his personality on the phone was completely different than the man I met in person. He was full of life, and I was excited.

The publisher sent me a questionnaire in which I needed to add the outline of the book. *Ha, I don't have an outline of the book*, I thought. *I have an idea for a book.* Then it hit me: I wanted to build the chapters around the social media posts I'd been writing. I laid them out on the floor and arranged them how they made sense to me, and there was an outline for the book. I sent the questionnaire back with the outline and synopsis.

"Go write," the publishers told me.

"Excuse me, would you like to share how I should write?"

"No, go write."

Write I did.

I wanted to add other voices to the book, so I created a questionnaire and asked people I knew and those I didn't know to fill it out. When people started hearing about the questionnaires and asking if they could fill them out, I knew I was on to something. Employees had something to say to company leadership.

I also wanted to have a small chapter on global DEI, and I found out that international corporations, businesses, and governments were focused on gender and disability. They would say there were no race issues, yet speaking with employees of color, that was clearly not the case.

Then, while writing the book, COVID shut down the world.

A few weeks into the pandemic, I began receiving calls and emails asking about how to manage stress. Friends and colleagues know I'm a chaplain, and people were struggling. The problem was that I was spending my days having the same conversation repeatedly. By the end of April, I reached out to a colleague with whom I had moderated a panel just before the pandemic. We had discussed doing something together in the future, and that future was now. I asked him if he would be interested in collaborating with me to hold a webinar. I explained how I was receiving so many calls and emails and that I needed a single space where I could respond to everyone. Additionally, it would provide people with the chance to talk and see one another.

I invited my friends and a few others to join me for the webinar, choosing a topic about navigating the crisis. I was shocked by the number of people who attended. I decided it would be a weekly webinar; I selected the topics based on suggestions, always with a focus on how to move forward in this uncertain world. Men and women of various ages and ethnicities participated. One woman even set her clock in India to wake up and join us, which humbled me. The weekly gathering became a forum for sharing without judgment. The webinar was something different—yet another medium for connection and healing, unique to what I had experienced before.

Then, the world shook once more. But this time, it was still rotating from the last shake, as we were still on lockdown. George Floyd was murdered, and it was filmed for everyone to see. There was no mistake: He yelled that he couldn't breathe, and the officer kept his knee on Floyd's neck. There was no mistake: He called out for his mother, and the officer kept his knee on Floyd's neck as he lay there and died for all to see, as other officers watched.

However you feel about what happened, you can't deny the above.

All of a sudden, my phone and email were going berserk. I barely had time to digest what I had witnessed when the calls came in: "How do you feel?" or, "I'm so sorry," or, "That just isn't right."

I had to be the one to say, "This is not the first Black man killed when there were alternatives; this is not new. It may be new to you because we were all in lockdown for the first time, picked our heads up, and saw beyond our current culture."

My book, *Expand Beyond Your Current Culture*, was writing itself.

I began receiving calls from past and present clients who were not sure how to navigate the conversations around the video, race, DEI, culture, and community. So many companies had already failed in the way they handled COVID with their employees; now, they *really* didn't know what to do.

The knee-jerk reaction was to put out a statement. Most executives were being pressured by their employees to say something or do something. I turned down the requests to write statements, except for two companies. Most calls I received seemed like performative actions: "Our competition said something, and now we need to say something." No plan, no action. Just a post.

I did consult for one company that I had worked with in the past; I knew they meant what they wanted to say. The other request I accepted was from a company that wanted a statement on Black Lives Matter and an action plan. I worked with their PR team, in-house attorneys, and executives to ensure that there was not only a plan but also the people in place to execute it. Then they brought me in to discuss the plan with the entire staff of both companies.

During this time, I was working from 6:00 a.m. to 10:00 p.m. with both national and international companies that wanted to make sense of what was happening in the States. I worked with educational, corporate, and not-for-profit organizations and had speaking engagements on "I Don't See Color (Please Do)." I also worked with multiple clients on building inclusive spaces, understanding what DEI means, and learning why it's essential to build company culture beyond your pizza parties. I was busy!

What people didn't realize was that events like this were and are far too familiar in Black communities. I was trying to help others make sense of it—not for pity, but for understanding outside of those Black communities—and the demand for this work was overwhelming. Many days, I had twenty minutes to eat before being back on a Zoom call.

As so many sought my help, so many others dismissed my experience. I never thought I would need to say "I am Black" as much as I did after George Floyd's murder. I asked my neighbors if they could hear me because I felt like I was screaming "I'm Black!" every hour. I thought it was obvious. Still, many people said or thought, "Well, not you, Leslie," meaning I did not have to deal with what the "other" Black people dealt with. I had privilege and privileges.

I would say, "That is true to some extent, but I'm Black! I still deal with many of the same things the 'others' have to."

People must decide how comfortable they are with you and your color. I've always heard, "Oh no, not you, Leslie." This has always been my moment to openly ask, "What do you see, and how do you perceive people? Who are you, and what value can you add to this conversation if you haven't taken the time to listen—if you aren't willing to engage with issues you may not fully understand?"

I conducted a workshop primarily with white women, and while I don't remember what I asked, I distinctly recall that they began to cry. I went from a full screen of faces to none—many had turned their cameras off. I paused and said, "If you want to be part of the solution, crying isn't it." When they returned, I asked, "Do you realize that I don't have the luxury or privilege to cry? My job, which I love, is being tested, as I desperately want you to see people for who they are, not as what you want or believe they should be. I'm asking you to take a breath and educate yourselves on Black history. I'll answer any questions you have, as long as I know you're putting in the effort."

I communicated the same thing the following month during our discussion on Asian hate. Because I have lived outside of the States, I have a sensibility towards culture and community, which made it easy for me to adapt our conversations and include other experts with lived experience and cultural expertise.

Suddenly, companies wanted to post (and did post) a black-colored box on social media, not understanding the context. Then, Juneteenth officially became a holiday, and companies started saying, "Now we hire Black people. Where are the Black people?"

I would get the calls saying, "Help us hire Black and brown people" (though they really meant Black people).

My first question would be, "Why?"

Most didn't have an answer.

I would then respond, "Please do not hire Black or Brown people; your culture is not ready."

I would ask, "What does diversity mean to you? Equity? Inclusion? If diversity only means race, then you are wrong; if equity only means money, you are wrong; and if inclusion is only for Black and Brown folks in the room, you are wrong."

Many colleagues were mad at me. I didn't care. It was not about hiring Black and Brown folks. If they got in but the culture was not one where they could succeed, then it would be too easy to say they were not ready or that DEI didn't work.

The other issue was that suddenly, everyone was labeled a DEI expert by default. If you were Black or Brown, you were now in charge of DEI. Most people filling those positions only had their lived experience, and that is not the work. I would shout, "Diversity is race, gender, LGBTQ+, disabilities sightseen and unseen, and veterans. You need to speak about the above and understand laws, policies, programs, data, and business. Then you need the buy-in and support of the executives in the company." Having a budget and staff would also help because simply throwing cultural lunches and holidays does not show a diverse individual coming into a company how they can be successful in a workplace where most of the employees do not walk like them, talk like them, and aren't them.

After George Floyd, I spent three years working with the education district in New York. In addition to being a guest teacher and keynote speaker, I was written in as part of a three-year grant to hold workshops with K–8th grade teachers. We had ninety minutes a week for ten weeks, with a different topic each time we met to build trust with teachers, counselors, and parents. Not all the teachers cared about representation, the meaning of words, or classroom culture. It was a different way of conducting workshops, and it pushed me to break things down differently. I loved the teacher who didn't agree but told me she liked me, even while still questioning why she should change. I loved the teacher who shared that she took my advice and allowed her class to share how they wanted to be represented. She said it changed not only how the students related to each other but also the parents.

When I give a workshop, keynote, or consultation, my job is not to make you think like me. My job is to open up a conversation where you may see a different way of looking at something, even if you still don't agree with it. That's called diversity of thinking: hearing something that you may not completely agree with but seeing how it can enhance a situation and move you forward for the betterment of the whole, not just self.

When I work with companies on DEI, I always explain that when we review the company, it must be from the mailroom to the boardroom. You cannot pick and choose where you think representation matters. If you are building an inclusive culture, then it's in the foundation of how you review your company internally and externally. I am happy to work with companies that understand and do the work to maintain this kind of culture.

The importance of diverse thinking was the message I planned on sharing at my book release on January 15, 2021. But after January 6th and the storming of the United States Capitol, I lost interviews. The conversation of the moment was no longer about culture, DEI, or the workplace; it was about politics.

It took a moment for the topic of conversation to focus back on the workplace. While I was working with clients around that time, I started receiving calls from news stations inviting me to contribute to discussions about the culture shift in companies. Those discussions were moving in the direction of hiring along with reviewing branding and messaging. The message of "representation matters" returned as a rallying cry.

Around that same time, I received a message on LinkedIn that a company was looking for a Black podcaster and that I should submit my podcast. I laughed, thanked the person who sent me the message, and told them I only had my COVID webinar, not a podcast. She told me to reach out anyway. I thought, *What do I have to lose?*

I reached out to the company to find out what the requirements were. I repeated the same thing I had told my friend: "I have a webinar series, not a podcast."

The podcast agency said, "If you have recorded the webinar, you have a podcast."

Visibility Ultd. was born that day—after I asked for help, because I had no idea how to turn the webinar into a podcast or where to begin. I did get accepted by the podcast agency, but they took too long to get off the ground, so I did what I do, and I kept it moving. Luckily, the same person who started the webinar series with me knew all about podcasts and helped kick off what is now a once-a-month podcast release covering topics around social impact, culture, DEI, business, and current events. I highlight topics and people you may not always hear about or from, and we get different perspectives on everyday cultural and business topics.

Unfortunately, four years later, DEI is still under attack. It's under attack because companies didn't implement it in a sustainable and comprehensible way. I am sorry to see colleagues closing their businesses and having to make full career shifts because we have become a country where, if you don't agree with the way someone thinks, then your perspective doesn't matter to them. Regardless, I know that having diverse talent is profitable. I am happy I have always focused on culture through a DEI lens, and I will continue to do so.

In 2022, I was hired by two different companies. I did my homework on them as they did on me. I saw an excellent opportunity to help them build and expand their culture. I met with the companies' executives, owners, and staff. As is normally the case, staff had different views from the executives in both companies. No surprise.

The bottom line was that everyone wanted to see movement. We built DEI committees with an interview process, set goals, conducted surveys, shared recaps, and planned on starting with what I call low-hanging fruit. Certain policy changes and inclusive language changes in a company don't cost much.

However, I began to notice that when I asked to speak with the CEOs I was told I had access to, I was blocked. My emails would go unanswered, yet the invoices were being paid. Finally, after speaking to the CEOs from both companies, I realized what was happening. It was nice to say in their clubhouse, "I have a

DEI expert," but they did not want to do the work. One even told me he didn't care about other religious holidays or LGBTQ+ representation because it was against his values. When I hear things like that, I say a silent prayer for the wisdom to share words of clarity and understanding.

"Your values mean a lot to you, and I understand," I responded, "but you opened your company doors. People came to work and expected that their values would be respected too. Because you didn't say, nor in your company values did you mention, that everyone must think the same as you."

By the end of the call, I thanked him for sharing his honest values with me. The more honest he was with me, the more I realized what he could be saying about me behind closed doors. I thanked him again and said I'd like to let the committee and staff know that I was not best suited to work with the company.

I was honest when I told the committee that I was not the best fit, but deep down, they knew something else had happened. I received emails from staff once they heard I had left. I was grateful for the connections I had made with them—but sad to see that the company would continue to lose good people because the owner simply didn't care. The turnover rate was like nothing I had ever seen before.

I have since expanded my services to do much more. I aim to help people understand that inclusivity transcends workshops and ADA (Americans with Disabilities Act) requirements, encompassing both visible and invisible disabilities. For the past three years, I've worked as an Accessibility Officer for TV and film productions. I enjoy this work, utilizing all my skills, and particularly my conflict resolution abilities.

I once worked on a show where a runner insisted that the door positioned behind the ramp needed to be open, even though there was no need for celebrities to exit the stage that way. I made it clear that everyone would exit using the side steps unless they had a disability or injury. In those cases, they would be escorted in front of the stage and exit through the opposite side door—the same one used to access the press room.

Despite this, the runner approached me at least three times, insisting that the ramp had to be moved. My silent prayer for patience was wearing thin. I finally looked at her and, with a slightly raised voice, said, "If you come to me one more time about removing the ramp, you and I will have a personal issue. Stop telling me who you spoke to. I'm making the final decision on the ramp's placement. The CEO is aware of it, and the final walkthrough happened yesterday. Thank you for your concern, but I believe it's misplaced, and certainly not focused on anyone who might actually need the ramp."

People often ask why I'm such an advocate for accessibility. "Do you have a family member with a disability?" they'll ask. The answer is no. But if I'm committed to inclusion and culture, then accessibility must be part of that conversation. It's not optional.

As I write this, I'm enrolled in an American Sign Language (ASL) class. I learned the ASL alphabet when I was younger, and it's a skill I always wanted to learn, but classes were far away or expensive when I searched for them. I was pleased when I saw a Facebook post from someone in my neighborhood saying that if anyone was interested, there might be an opportunity to start a local class. I jumped at the chance. I practice, and I host a study group on Sundays. It's hard, but I made a promise to one of the actors who is deaf that the next time I worked with him, I would be able to say more than "hi" and "thank you." I'm not trying to be an interpreter; I just want to be able to hold a simple conversation.

I have learned a lot about deaf culture. What I know, and what we all need to know, is that no matter how much you study, learn, and immerse yourself in a culture, it is still not your culture. Stop trying to be an ally—be a champion or advocate with respect. I hope that is what I am doing for all the communities and cultures I speak and teach about.

So much was happening through COVID, as I counted big wins and deep losses. Business wise, I was in a groove. My business flourished. Yet at the same time, the number of people who passed and how that was handled was horrible. I lost my boxing coach to COVID. There were funerals I could not attend, and I held virtual funerals for friends' parents who passed. It was rough, and I struggled to understand: *How can I be joyful for one thing while so many people and other things are crumbling around me?*

My friend asked me to handle her mother's virtual service and help her with the process, for which I will always feel honored. Others asked me as well. During virtual funerals, it was hard to look at people's faces in boxes and know they wanted to be together but couldn't. After the service, I would close my screen and allow them time together. I couldn't imagine finishing the service and cutting off the Zoom.

I would often take walks past the hospital where I had been the interim chaplain and say a prayer for all who worked there and all that had to take place there. I would see the outside trailers used for morgues. I couldn't imagine what that was like. I'd had to go to the morgue several times as chaplain, taking families there to see their loved ones if they did not make it to the hospital in time. It's not a place you want to take someone. It's not a place that should be outside in trailers. But that was where we were, and all I could do was walk on the side of the street without barriers and pray.

No matter how many funerals I help with or conduct, I know my path is being guided. Do I think I should have stayed in seminary? No. I believe God called me to serve in exactly the way that was planned for me.

EPILOGUE

What Is Happening?

I don't say I'm lucky; I say I'm blessed. Blessed with opportunity, and even more blessed to recognize it when it shows up.

Dancing took me around the world—twice. And even while owning businesses or running them for others, I kept moving, kept traveling. My friends laugh when I claim dual nationality. It's our inside joke, but it's true. I'm always ready to go in the blink of an eye.

I love the work I do. Every chapter, every shift, has shaped who I am. So, when someone questions your path—asks why you're studying that subject, taking that course, or stepping into something new where no one else in your circle has gone—just smile. Keep moving. Someone has to be the first.

I've been blessed, and my bumps in the road are just that compared to so many stories I have heard and witnessed. I work hard and enjoy life. When I see so many people suffering and those in charge unwilling or uninterested in helping—unless the people who need help are in the same group as them—it makes me question what's going on.

As I write the title of this chapter, I honestly wonder what is happening to the world. An industry that is messy at best, but needed and beneficial to all when done correctly, is being politicized and attacked as harmful. Diversity, Equity, and Inclusion are not bad terms, together or separately.

I keep receiving calls asking if I'm okay.

Yes, I'm okay because I focus on culture, and if that's done correctly, DEI will be embedded in a company's DNA.

Yes, I'm okay, but it's painful seeing colleagues close their firms because they no longer have contracts.

A publicist asked me why I was not on TV again as a news contributor, as I was during the pandemic and after George Floyd's murder.

"There is too much noise, and people are not ready to listen; they just want to point fingers," I responded. "I don't need to be part of a conversation that simply points fingers; I'm here to share solutions."

Companies that have decided to "get rid" of DEI cannot put the genie back in the bottle. You can take away groups and cultural gatherings, but you cannot take away someone's culture. You cannot take away the fact that people want to and have the right to live their lives as they see fit. I will always and have always stood up for those who need strength in numbers to elevate themselves or a cause that has proven to benefit us all.

So . . .

What is happening? I am not sure.

But I know that no matter what happens, I will stay true to who I am. No one can or will steal my joy. I will continue to learn. I will continue to expand beyond my current culture. I will continue to explore the world.

No matter what happens, I will make sure to tell friends and loved ones I love them. I will continue to work out. I will stand in my womanism as it fits my body. I will keep eating sour gummy worms. I will continue to be the friend who has wine and cheese on call.

No matter what happens, I will continue to work. I will continue to fight the good fight. I will not define you unless you ask me to. I will stand in my Blackness as it is designed for me. Anyone else's thoughts or opinions will not define me.

No matter what happens, my voice will be used for good. I will stand strong in my faith. I will try to do no harm.

No matter what happens, if the opportunity arises for me to be the first and it makes sense to me, then I will take it. I will continue to celebrate all the firsts who came before me and those who will come after.

If you take nothing else from my story, I hope you know you always have options. They may not be the options you think you want or deserve, but having options is power; you are powerful and privileged! Our privileges don't make us better, but they give us opportunities we must not waste.

Follow your gut and be true to who you are. Live out loud, whatever that means to you.

Keep in mind that someone has to be the first. And if it's you, keep the doors open so you're not the last!

Acknowledgments

I give all my love to my parents, Gothrie and Mae, my sister, Sheri, and my nephew, Michael. I know you are sick of hearing me say I need to write. The support you have shown me throughout my life is unspeakable. I would have achieved none of this without you!

To my Aunties: I love you to the moon and back! I send love to my cousins.

Cousin Sandy, you still need to make up for the time you lied to me when we were kids and said piercing your ears didn't hurt, then cried after I had my first one pierced!

To everyone who has the title of being the first, I understand that wasn't your purpose, but it is your faith. Thank you for paving the way for me to earn my first. I look forward to others claiming their first too.

To those with whom my path has crossed for a moment, a day, or a week, the crossing was purposeful. Thank you for sharing that time with me.

My friends, some of you have rolled with me in the US and some outside of the States. Thank you for the shenanigans, laughter, tears, wine, cheese, chocolate, and gummies. More than that, thank you for the support. You have watched me change careers, build companies, and most of all, keep it moving. You have never faltered, even when you thought I was nuts for going in a new direction. I love you!

Dwayne, for every, "Hey, look at what I'm doing. Would you like to read it over? Can you read it over? I forgot to tell you I'm . . ." you laugh and say, "Please send it." You have watched out for me and my businesses, and you have been a friend through it all.

Anne, Susan, and Dianna, a.k.a. NNA, we have stories we can't write about!

Tyler and Tiffany, shenanigans—and I wouldn't trade one of them.

Mark, from New York to Japan and back, I love you!

I have had the most amazing clients, and I want to thank you for allowing me to be myself while working alongside you.

Paolo, I had no idea you were in the audience during my speaking engagement, and I didn't realize you had added me to the list of Forbes' "Black Women to Watch" not once, but twice or even three times.[1] Who knew that a coffee to officially say hello and thank you would lead to you becoming one of my partners in crime in the DEI and culture space.

Thank you to every consultant who went through the K.I.M. Media LLC boot camp. You will never know how much means to me when you come back from working an event and call to tell

---

1 Paulo Gaudiano, "More Awesome Black Women Everyone Should Know," Forbes, February 26, 2020, https://www.forbes.com/sites/paologaudiano/2020/02/26/more-awesome-black-women-everyone-should-know/.

me, "Well, that was not a K.I.M. Media production."

My FUBU guys, Keith, Carl, J, and Daymond—and of course Grim—I appreciate you.

Beth and Ms. Haught, I wish I knew where you were so I could thank you for recognizing what you saw in me at seven. I hope I've made you proud. To all the dance teachers and choreographers I've worked with, thank you.

Special thanks to Theo, Richard, and Victor for your Spirit and Blessings.

David, let's live life and not let life live us.

My Philly Crew, Geoff, Bob, Maree, Roxanne, Angela, and Amanda—aghhhhhh, The Village.

Special thank you to Tony Rahsaan, Joe Pryor, Lynne Filderman, Barbara Matos, Elena Romero, Ethelie Aruoture, Grace Lee, Kim Smith, Colin Williams, Stanley Debase, Emi Kirschner, Lana Walker, Laurel Getz, Anna Williams, Leana Parhami Shayefar, Joyce Dugger, Julia Moore, Donnie Fox, and Dolores Concepcion.

To God, thank you for allowing me to work for you later in life, heels and all! I am grateful for each day, every challenge, and every opportunity.

About the Author

Leslie Short is a former ballet dancer turned corporate operations strategist, dedicated to helping businesses build and sustain inclusive workplace cultures.

A chaplain, activist, certified mental health aide, mediator, and conflict coach, Leslie is also a sought-after international speaker who has addressed audiences at the United Nations, the European Union, and beyond.

She is the founder and owner of K.I.M. Media LLC, Ascend Bereavement Management, and The Cavu Group, as well as the author of *Expand Beyond Your Current Culture*. With more than four decades of experience as a brand and culture strategist and leadership advisor, Leslie established The Cavu Group to design workplace strategies and facilitate transformative discussions that push organizations to move beyond the status quo.

Her achievements have been widely recognized, earning honors such as *Outstanding Woman in Marketing & Communications, Woman of Influence,* and the *Top 50 Impact of Power* award.

Leslie's passions include the arts in all forms—music, dance, fashion—and a lifelong commitment to learning. She is also the host of the *Visibility Ultd.* podcast.

www.ingramcontent.com/pod-product-compliance
Lightning Source LLC
LaVergne TN
LVHW091040080826
845145LV00002B/570